PANFISH

THE HUNTING & FISHING LIBRARY

By Dick Sternberg and Bill Ignizio

DICK STERNBERG, formerly a professional fisheries biologist, writes in a style that features a unique blend of scientific knowledge and angling experience.

BILL IGNIZIO, a teacher in outdoor education, has authored numerous panfish articles for magazines throughout the country.

CREDITS:

Project Director: Dick Sternberg
Editorial Director: Chuck Wechsler
Production Director: Christine Watkins
Art Directors: Cy DeCosse, Delores Swanson
Director of Photography: Buck Holzemer
Staff Photographers: Brian Berkey, Bill Lindner, Jerry Robb
Project Managers: Cindy Hawker, Elizabeth Woods
Chief Researcher: Joseph Cella
Researchers: Lowell Holland, Teresa Marrone, Jay Strangis
Production Staff: Michelle Alexander, Gail Bailey, Jim Bindas, Diane Johnson, Mary Ann Knox, Christopher Lentz, Tim Minkkinen, Nancy Nardone, Tom Nordby, Don Oster, Gregory Schaffner, Jennie Smith, Ellen Sorenson, Donna Mae Tomashek, Leo Torola
Contributing Photographers: Bruce Arneson, Roger W. Barbour, Tommie A. Berger, Graham Brown, W. Horace Carter, Joseph Cella, Jack Fallon, Curt Johnson, Anthony Kubat, Jerry Krause, Michael Maceina, Steve McHugh, Ron Morreim, Nebraska Game and Parks Commission, C. Boyd Pfeiffer, John E. Phillips, William Roston, Doug Stamm, Dick Sternberg, Jay Strangis, Allan Tarvid, Conrad Vollertsen, Chuck Wechsler, Wisconsin Department of Natural Resources — Bureau of Research
Special Consultants: Joe Ehrhardt, Steve Price, Bill Schieman
Consultants: Parker Bauer; Larry Belusz, Missouri Department of Conservation; Curt Carpenter; W. Horace Carter; Mike Fennel; Dr. John Forney, Cornell University Biological Field Station; Robert Foye, Maine Department of Inland Fisheries and Wildlife; Elmer Guerri; Bob Hidle; Tom Huggler; Wallace Johnson; Michael Maceina, Center for Aquatic Weeds; Steve McCadams; Jon Poehler; LeRoy Ras; Frank Sargeant; Jim Seabolt; Duane Shodeen, Minnesota Department of Natural Resources; Ernest Simmons, Texas Parks and Wildlife Department; Art Singer; Nick Sisley; Bill Thomas; Louis Vogele, Aquatic Ecosystem Analysts; Charles Waterman; Rich Zaleski
Cooperating Agencies and Individuals: A.C. Shiners, Inc.; Fred Arbogast Company, Inc.; Arctic Fisherman; Ardisam, Inc.; Arnold Tackle Corporation; Jim Bagley Bait Co., Inc.; Carl Baker, Ohio Department of Natural Resources; Harold Barber; Bead Chain Tackle Co.; Jerry Benson; Betts Tackle, Ltd.; Blakemore Sales Corp.; Mike Bleech; Don Bonneau, Jim Mayhew, R. H. McWilliams, Iowa State Conservation Commission; Bright Waters, Inc.; Brinkmann Corporation; Stan Bular, Jim Kalkofen, Mariner Outboards; Burger Brothers Sporting Goods; Burke Fishing Lures; Frank Calistro; Lew Childre & Sons, Inc.; Mike and Dan Chimelak; Homer Circle; Coleman Co., Inc.; A.J. Collier; Michael Colvin, Missouri Department of Conservation; Comet Tackle Company; Cordell Tackle; Norm Crawford; Creme Lure Company; Larry Dahlberg; Daiwa Corporation; Bob Daly, D&D Electronics, Inc.; Claude Davis; Chuck DeNoto; Dickey Tackle Company; Dot Lure, Inc.; Dura-Pak Corporation; Frankie Dusenka and Dick Grzywinski, Frankie's Live Bait; Eppinger Manufacturing Co.; Stan Fagerstrom; Jack Fallon; Fenwick-Woodstream Corp.; Ed Fieler, Howard Krosch, Jack Skrypek, Minnesota Department of Natural Resources; Lewis Flagg, Maine Department of Marine Resources; Dr. Calvin Fremling, Winona State University; Jerry Fuller, Fuller's Tackle; Dan Gapen; Gaines Company; Raymond Gauthier; Paul Grahl, HT Enterprises; Grassl's Double 00, Inc.; Grumman Boats; Hal-Fly Tackle Co., Inc.; Carl Hamilton; James Heddon's Sons, Inc.; Mark Hicks; Bob Hobson, Alumacraft Boat Co.; Warren Hollier; Hopkins Fishing Lures Co., Inc.; George Huber; Bill James, Indiana Department of Natural Resources; Joanie Jiggs Co.; Johnson Fishing, Inc.; Jungle Laboratories Corporation; Kentucky Department of Fish and Wildlife Resources; Clem Koehler, Mercury Marine; Bob Knopf, Berkley and Company, Inc.; Lake Country Products; LAKEMAPS-Diversified Design, Inc.; Paul Liikala; Jim Lindner, The In-Fisherman Magazine; Lindy-Little Joe, Inc.; Lowrance Electronics, Inc.; Luhr Jensen & Sons, Inc.; Ray Matousek; Jane Memke, Polaris Industries, Inc.; Mepp's; Michigan Department of Natural Resources; Mister Twister, Inc.; Pat Mitchell; Jim Moore, Lund American, Inc.; Bill Neal, Virginia Commission of Game and Inland Fisheries; John Nickum, Iowa Cooperative Fisheries Research Unit; Tom Nixon; OMC-Evinrude; Orvis Co., Inc.; Leo Pachner, Farm Pond Harvest; Ed Park; Penn Fishing Tackle Mfg. Co.; Ged Petit, Tennessee Wildlife Resources Agency; C. Boyd Pfeiffer; Maria Quinn; Ranger Boats; Roy's Live Bait; Ryobi America Corp.; Sage-Winslow Mfg. Corp; Bill Scifres; Block Sexton; Shakespeare Fishing Tackle Division; Barry Smith, Alabama Department of Conservation and Natural Resources; Smithwick Lures, Inc.; Hurschel Snider; Sorel Boots-Sports Sales Inc.; Glen Steel; Storm Manufacturing Co.; Tennessee Valley Authority; Claude Titus; Jim Tomlinson; Umpqua Feather Merchants, Inc.; Uncle Josh Bait Co.; VMC, Inc.; Vexilar, Inc.; Marvin Walls, Angler's Sport Center, Ltd.; Calvin J. Wingate; Wisconsin Department of Natural Resources; Wright and McGill Co.; Zebco Division, Brunswick Corp.; Joe Zemnicki
Color Separations: Weston Engraving Co., Inc.
Printing: Moebius Printing Co.

Also available from the publisher: *The Art of Freshwater Fishing, Cleaning & Cooking Fish, Fishing With Live Bait, Largemouth Bass.*

Contents

Introduction

Many an accomplished fisherman mastered his angling basics as a youngster catching crappies in a small lake or bluegills in a farm pond. But panfish angling is not just for kids. Big panfish, like the 2-pound crappie shown life-size on these pages, offer an exciting challenge for any fisherman.

Anglers across the country catch staggering numbers of panfish. No other type of fish comes even close in terms of numbers caught. In a recent year, fishermen on one southern reservoir caught over 2 million panfish, including 1.5 million crappies.

It's easy to understand why panfish are so popular. They live in every type of water, from 1-acre ponds to 100,000-acre lakes. Most kinds bite throughout the year and you can catch them without a lot of expensive equipment. They wage a scrappy battle on light tackle and are tops on the dinner table.

In this book, the term *panfish* includes gamefish that never outgrow the size of a frying pan. Although some writers include larger fish like catfish, walleyes and pickerel, these species will appear in future volumes of *The Hunting & Fishing Library*.

In the first section, we explain how to select your fishing

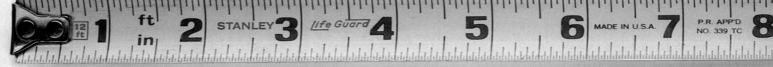

equipment, from ultralight rods and telescopic poles to slip-bobbers and casting bubbles. You will learn the basics of fly-casting, one of the most exciting panfish techniques.

The most popular species, including sunfish, crappies, white bass and yellow perch, receive thorough coverage in separate sections. Another section features panfish that are popular in certain regions, like white perch and rock bass. It even includes some lesser-known types like the Rio Grande and Sacramento perch.

You will discover the habits of panfish based on research by the nation's leading fisheries biologists. And you will learn the best angling techniques from experts around the country. We encourage you to experiment with the tips and techniques in this book, then devise a fishing strategy that suits your waters. Many of the techniques featured for one type of fish can be used to catch other panfish species. Some of the rigs, baits and methods may be illegal in your state. If you have any doubt, check with local authorities first.

The ice-fishing section traces panfish movements over the winter months and recommends the best baits and techniques. We will share some little-known tips that make ice fishing more comfortable and productive.

This book will help you catch good-sized panfish, *consistently*. Expert anglers know that plate-sized bluegills, slab crappies and jumbo perch can be just as elusive as trophy bass, trout and walleyes. This book provides the specific information you need to catch big panfish in a variety of waters, throughout the year.

Rods & Reels

You can catch panfish on almost any rod and reel, but with light tackle, even a half-pound sunfish can wage a respectable fight.

Light, open-face spinning tackle is a good all-around choice. For casting extremely light lures, such as a 1/32-ounce jig, an ultralight rod works better.

But a rod that is too flexible, or *slow*, lacks sensitivity, and makes it difficult to set the hook.

Many fishermen use closed-face spinning gear because they believe the push-button reel is more tangle-free and easier to cast than open-face tackle. Several manufacturers make small spin-cast outfits designed mainly for panfish angling.

When fishing in timber, brush, dense weeds or other snaggy cover, you need heavier gear to pull the

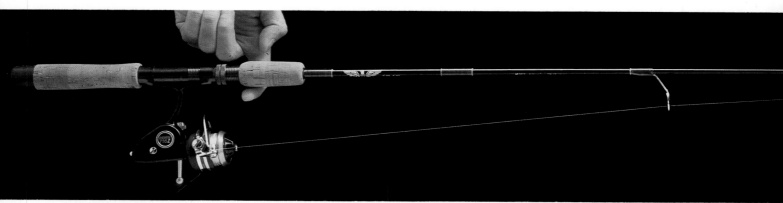

ALL-PURPOSE RODS for panfish have light to medium power, measure 4½ to 5½ feet, and weigh only 2 to 4 ounces. Many panfish experts prefer graphite or boron rods because they are lighter and more sensitive than fiberglass. But high-quality fiberglass rods work almost as well. The guides and tip should be lined with

MULTIPLE EXPOSURE PHOTOGRAPH

FAST-ACTION rods (left) bend mainly near the tip. They work best for detecting strikes and setting the hook. A medium-action rod (right) is more flexible. It will bend, or *load,* enough to cast even a tiny lure.

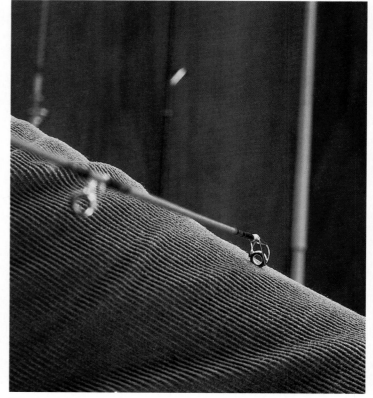

SENSITIVITY depends on rod material and action. To determine sensitivity, rub the tip of the rod lightly across corduroy. With a sensitive rod, you can feel the texture of the material.

hook free of obstructions. Many fishermen use medium power spinning or bait-casting equipment.

Cane poles or telescopic fiberglass poles work well for dropping bait into tight spots and pulling fish straight up out of weeds or brush. Some anglers prefer stout flippin' rods designed for bass fishing.

A fly rod is the best choice for casting poppers, hair bugs and other surface lures. It also works for presenting streamers, wet flies and nymphs.

Many anglers believe that fly-fishing is too difficult. But most fishermen can learn the basic casting techniques with only a few hours of practice.

The overhead cast (page 10) works well in most situations. When an obstruction interferes with your backcast, use the roll cast (page 11).

You do not need a fly rod for casting fly lures. Spinning tackle with a casting bubble for extra weight works equally well.

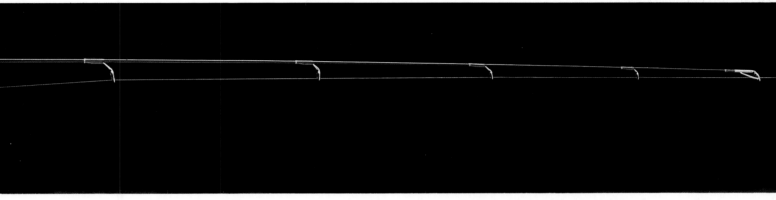

aluminum oxide, silicon carbide, or some other hard material. Soft materials will become grooved from repeated casting and fray the line. To determine whether

your reel matches the rod, balance the rod on your finger just ahead of the reel. If the outfit is properly balanced, the rod will rest in a horizontal position.

CANE POLES or telescopic fiberglass poles should be stiff enough to hoist fish out of openings in cover. Most anglers use 12- to 16-foot poles, then tie on a length of

monofilament several feet longer than the pole. Some extension poles have built-in reels. The angler threads the line through the inside of the pole and out the tip.

FLY RODS for panfish are usually 7 to 8 feet long and designed for No. 5 or No. 6 fly lines. Experienced fly fishermen use lightweight rods made of graphite or boron. The number of guides should equal the rod's

length; an 8-foot rod should have eight guides. If the rod does not have enough guides, the line will sag between the guides, creating extra friction and reducing your casting distance.

STRIP about 25 feet of line from your reel and allow it to fall to the water. Hold the line in one hand and the rod in the other. With the rod parallel to the water, slowly raise the tip to pick up the slack.

BEGIN the backcast by lifting the rod with a gradually accelerating motion. Stop the rod at the 11 o'clock position. This motion will lift the line from the water and throw it back over your shoulder.

PAUSE long enough for the line to straighten out behind you. As soon as you feel a slight tug, begin the forward cast. If you start too soon, you will lose leverage and the line will fall onto the water in coils.

MOVE the rod forward with a smooth downward stroke, gradually slowing the motion as the loop of line unrolls. The line should be straight as it lands softly. For extra distance, strip more line and continue the casting motion, but keep the line in the air. This technique is called *false casting*. Let the line land when you reach your target.

How to Roll Cast

BEGIN a roll cast with 20 to 25 feet of line on the water in front of your body. Hold the rod parallel to the surface, then move it back over your shoulder to pick up slack. Stop the rod at 11 o'clock.

THRUST the rod forward with a powerful, downward stroke, then stop it at the 3 o'clock position. The line will form a large coil as it begins to unroll in the direction of the target.

KEEP the rod pointed at the target as the line continues to unroll. When cast properly, the line will follow a straight path.

Tips for Fly-casting

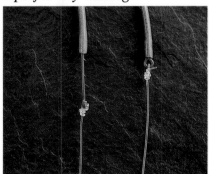

PUSH a barbed metal eyelet into the end of your fly line, then attach your leader to the eyelet.

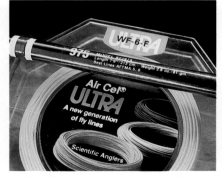

MATCH your line to the rod. For best casting performance, the line should be just heavy enough to load the rod.

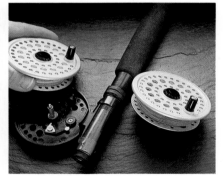

SELECT a fly reel with a snap-out spool. Then you can easily change lines for different situations.

Lines & Knots

The most common mistake in panfish angling is using line too heavy for the conditions. Four- to six-pound monofilament works best in most situations. Light line enables you to cast tiny lures and baits. And because of its smaller diameter, it sinks faster than heavy line, so you can reach bottom more easily. For casting extremely light baits, some fishermen use 2-pound mono.

Select limp mono when fishing with light lures or baits. Stiff line reduces casting distance and restricts the action of the lure or movement of the bait. Some panfish experts attach their lures with loop knots for added action.

Use a fly line that matches the line weight recommendations for your rod. A floating line works best most of the time. But to catch panfish in water deeper than 6 feet, you need a sinking or sinking-tip line. You can cast most panfish flies and bugs with a level line. However, a double taper allows for a more delicate presentation, because the end of the line has a smaller diameter. When one end wears out, reverse the line and use the other end.

A tapered mono leader offers the best casting performance. Some fishermen simply attach a length of plain monofilament. But mono does not unroll with the cast as well as a tapered leader. A 5X, or 3-pound test tippet works well for panfish. Most fishermen use 5- to 7-foot leaders. If casting a sinking line, use a shorter leader because it sinks quicker.

QUALITY mono is thinner for its strength than cheap line, so it is less visible to fish. High-grade fly line is more durable and easier to cast than inexpensive line.

The Loop Knot: Best for Small Lures

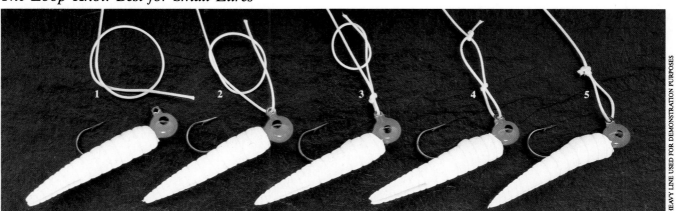

HEAVY LINE USED FOR DEMONSTRATION PURPOSES

TIE a loop knot by (1) making an overhand knot, then (2) passing the free end through the eye of the lure and back through the overhand knot. (3) Snug up the knot by pulling on the free end and standing line. Then tie another overhand knot around the standing line. (4) Snug up the second overhand knot and pull on the standing line to slide the two knots together. (5) Continue pulling until the two knots join, then trim the excess line.

Advantages of Light Line

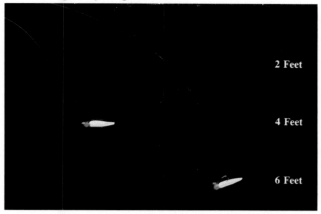

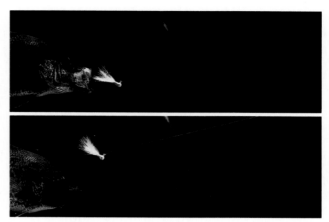

SINK RATE increases as the line weight decreases. A 1/16-ounce jig attached to 10-pound line (left) sinks only 4 feet in 3 seconds. But an identical jig (right) tied to 4-pound line sinks 6 feet.

LINE VISIBILITY can be important. In clear water, panfish are more likely to strike a jig tied to 4-pound monofilament (top) than a lure tied to 10-pound monofilament (bottom).

CASTING DISTANCE improves with lighter line because thin mono flows off the spool easily. These fishermen are using identical rods, reels and lures. The angler with 4-pound line (top) can cast 100 feet. The fisherman with 8-pound line (center) casts 80 feet. With 12-pound line (bottom), casting distance is only 60 feet.

Tips for Casting Light Lures

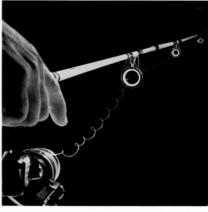

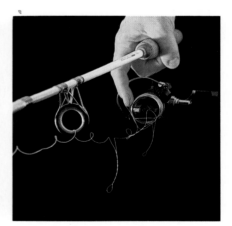

KEEP your spool filled to within 1/8-inch of the lip. If the level falls too low, line rubs on the lip, reducing your casting distance.

SELECT a spinning rod with large guides. Good-sized guides permit coils of line to flow through with a minimum of friction.

AVOID twisted line. Kinks interfere with line flow, and reduce casting distance. If they develop, trail the line behind the boat or spool on new line.

Terminal Tackle

The light rods, reels and lines used for panfish enable you to use light terminal tackle. With an ultra-light rod and 4-pound mono, you can easily cast a tiny bobber rig weighted with only a small split-shot.

Light terminal tackle makes it easy to detect a bite from a small fish. And once the fish takes the bait, it is not likely to feel resistance and spit the hook.

Many panfish anglers make the mistake of using a heavy leader. This will drastically reduce the number of bites and inhibit the action of your lure or bait. Tie your hook directly to the line, but check frequently for nicks or abrasions. Even the smallest scratch can cause 4-pound mono to break easily.

When fishing in brush, timber or other heavy cover, you need heavier terminal tackle. Some anglers use ½- to 1-ounce sinkers. When they become snagged, they shake the rod tip to bounce the sinker up and down, freeing the hook. But a heavy sinker requires a large bobber, so the fish can feel more resistance. With heavier tackle, you may have to set the hook at the first sign of a bite.

Popular Floats for Panfish

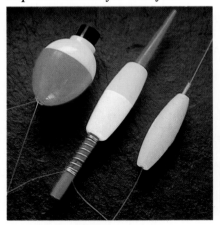

FIXED BOBBERS attach to the line in different ways. Widely used models include (left to right): clip-ons, spring-locks, peg bobbers.

CASTING BUBBLES sink slowly when filled with water. Adjust the speed of your retrieve to control the depth of the float.

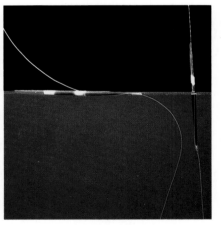

TIP-UP FLOATS like this quill bobber are the most sensitive. They lie flat on the water, then tip up when a fish takes the bait.

How to Select Panfish Hooks

HOOK SIZE depends on the size of the fish's mouth. Anglers use hooks as large as 2/0 for crappies and as small as #10 for sunfish.

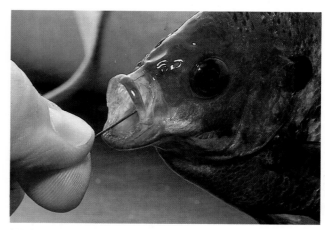

SHANK LENGTH is a matter of personal preference. Many fishermen prefer long-shank hooks because they are easiest to remove.

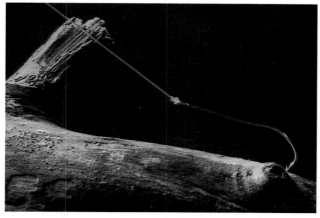

LIGHT-WIRE hooks work best in most situations. They do the least damage to small baits and will bend enough to pull free of snags.

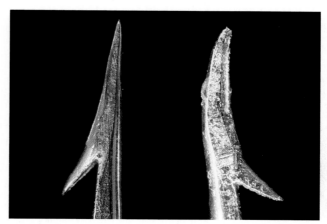

QUALITY hooks (left) have strong, sharp points. A cheap hook (right) is blunt and the soft metal point bends or breaks easily when fished on rocks.

How to Rig a Sliding Float

SELECT a float that slides easily, such as a (left) tube or (middle) cylinder float. Or use a (right) clip-on bobber set so the clip rests on the plastic.

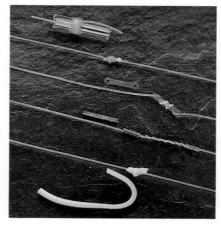

ATTACH a bobber stop at the depth you want to fish. You can buy several commercial types or simply tie a piece of rubber band to the line.

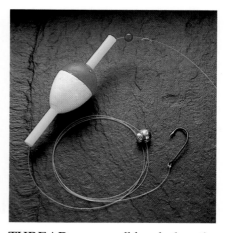

THREAD on a small bead, then the float. Tie on a hook, then add enough split-shot for balance about 8 inches up the line.

Anchors

Still-fishing from an anchored boat is the most popular panfish technique. But many fishermen make the mistake of anchoring near a school with an anchor that will not hold or a rope that is too short. When the anchor loses its grip, it drags through the school and scatters the fish.

Select an anchor with the right weight and design for your type of fishing. A 10-pound anchor may hold a low-profile jon boat, but it would not hold a deep semi-V, which has more wind resistance.

ANCHORS include: (1) Navy style which is best for strong wind or current, (2) mushroom and (3) river anchors which are adequate for most other situations, (4) brush clamp that can be used in place of an anchor.

How to Anchor in the Wind

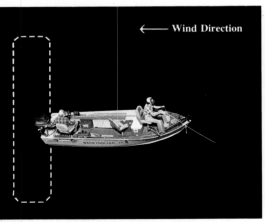

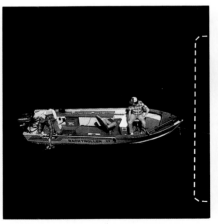

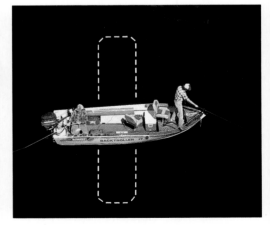

DROP one anchor upwind of the area you want to fish (dotted lines). The stronger the wind and deeper the water, the farther upwind you should anchor.

LOWER the second anchor after paying out enough of the first anchor rope for the boat to drift well downwind of your fishing spot.

MOVE the boat upwind into your fishing spot by pulling on the first anchor rope, while paying out the second line.

Other Equipment

Experienced panfish anglers prefer lively baits. To keep baitfish healthy, place them in a flow-through bucket or a styrofoam pail. You can keep worms in a can of black dirt, but they live longer and stay healthier if kept in a styrofoam container filled with worm bedding.

Chemical additives (page 67) can greatly prolong the lives of baitfish. Many bait shops sell oxygen tablets and battery-powered aerators to keep baitfish alive on the trip to your fishing spot.

The best insurance against dead bait is an ice chest. Worms, leeches, minnows, insect larvae and practically any other type of bait will live longer if kept cool. An ice chest also comes in handy for keeping your catch, especially in hot weather.

Many anglers keep their panfish in wire baskets. But in summer, warm surface temperatures may kill fish brought up from deeper, cooler water. Once a fish dies, it spoils rapidly in warm water. A fish kept on ice will stay fresh for eight hours or more.

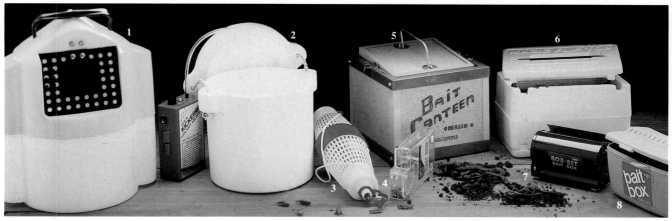

CONTAINERS for live bait include: (1) plastic flow-through minnow bucket, (2) styrofoam bucket with optional battery-powered aerator, (3 and 4) plastic dispensers for crickets and grasshoppers, (5) fiberboard worm container and (6) styrofoam worm box which allow oxygen to reach the worm bedding, (7) metal worm keeper and (8) plastic worm box which can be attached to the fisherman's belt.

Tips for Keeping Your Catch

KEEP your fish in a collapsible wire basket unless the water is too warm. Most baskets have a one-way, spring-loaded flap on top, so you can quickly drop in fish without letting any escape.

AVOID keeping panfish on a rope stringer, particularly during hot weather. Many fish die because their gills cannot work properly, and they tear off the stringer when you lift them from the water.

All About Sunfish

The name sunfish refers to the bright, sunny colors of these scrappy fighters. Throughout the South, fishermen refer to all sunfish as *bream* or *brim*. The names originated from early American settlers who thought the fish resembled a flat-bodied European species called a bream.

The sunfish family includes crappies, largemouth and smallmouth bass, rock bass and other fishes not called sunfish. But this chapter will include only true sunfish, members of the genus *Lepomis*.

The bluegill, redear, pumpkinseed, redbreast, warmouth, green and longear are the most popular sunfish. Many other types of true sunfish do not grow large enough to interest anglers. Species like spotted sunfish and dollar sunfish seldom reach 6 inches in length.

Different types of sunfish crossbreed, resulting in hybrids that have some characteristics of both parents. Hybrids may cross with other hybrids or with their parents. Even experienced biologists have trouble identifying fish from a hybridized population. Small hybrid sunfish are a nuisance in many lakes. But some hybrids are superior to the parent fish. For example, redear sunfish, when crossed with green sunfish, produce a fast-growing, hard-fighting hybrid.

Sunfish can adapt to almost any type of water, with the exception of cold lakes and streams. They live in small ponds, natural lakes, reservoirs and river backwaters. Most sunfish species seek out warm, shallow, slack-water areas. Some kinds, like the redbreast, prefer flowing water.

Most sunfish spawn from mid- to late spring. Some spawn several times at intervals throughout summer, which explains why anglers often catch egg-laden sunfish weeks after the spring spawning season. Spawning is normally completed by late July.

Sunfish have a strong homing instinct and return to spawn in the same vicinity each year. Prior to spawning, males choose a nest site (see table below), then use their tails to sweep the bottom clear of debris. The typical spawning bed measures 1 to 2 feet in diameter and several inches deep. The beds appear as round, light-colored spots on bottom. Sometimes the nests are so close together they form one massive spawning colony.

After depositing their eggs, females abandon the nests. The males remain for several days to guard the eggs and newly-hatched fry from predators.

Some species of sunfish produce so many young that they overpopulate a lake or pond. An individual spawning bed may contain as many as 200,000 fry. If a high percentage of young fish survive, they deplete their food supply, resulting in a population of stunted fish. Overpopulated lakes seldom produce keeper sunfish. The largest fish usually come from lakes with relatively low numbers of sunfish.

Most sunfish eat larval and adult insects, invertebrates, mollusks and small fish. They rely heavily on their senses of scent and sight to find food.

Sunfish usually feed in morning and early evening, but will also feed during midday. They will bite on sunny or cloudy days. Night fishing is best on clear nights with a bright moon, or around lighted docks.

Spawning Conditions for Sunfish

SPECIES	SPAWNING STARTS (AVG. WATER TEMP.)	PREFERRED BOTTOM TYPE	TYPICAL NESTING DEPTH
Bluegill	69°F	Sand or fine gravel	1 to 2½ feet
Redear	68°F	Softer bottoms in water lilies	1½ to 3 feet
Pumpkinseed	68°F	Sand or fine gravel	6 inches to 1½ feet
Redbreast	68°F	Sand or fine gravel	6 inches to 1½ feet
Warmouth	70°F	Small rock, lightly covered with silt	1½ to 4½ feet
Green	71°F	Gravel	6 inches to 1 foot
Longear	72°F	Gravel	6 inches to 2 feet

Bluegills

Bluegills are the most widespread and abundant sunfish species. They were originally found only in the eastern half of the United States, but stocking has expanded their range to include every state except Alaska.

Clear waters with moderate weed growth support the best bluegill populations. But they can also be found in murky lakes. Like most sunfish, they prefer warm, quiet waters. Some bluegills live in slow-moving portions of streams, but they rarely inhabit areas with swift current. They can tolerate slightly brackish water in estuaries.

As their name implies, bluegills have a powder blue gill cover. Females have yellow breasts; males copper-orange. The ear flap is entirely black. The bluegill has a black blotch on the lower rear of the dorsal fin, a mark not found on other sunfish. Bluegills in Florida waters usually have dark, vertical bars on their sides.

Although they grow larger than most other sunfish, bluegills seldom exceed 10 inches or 1 pound in size. Anglers commonly catch 6- to 9-inch bluegills. The world record, caught in Ketona Lake, Alabama in 1950, weighed 4 pounds, 12 ounces.

Bluegills feed primarily on insects, crustaceans and small fish. If other foods become scarce, they will eat aquatic vegetation. During midday, they may suspend to feed on tiny aquatic organisms, called plankton.

Bluegill Range

In laboratory tests, bluegills fed most heavily in 81-degree water. They did not feed when the water was below 50°F or above 88°F.

Redear Sunfish

Known as the *shellcracker* to most southern fishermen, the redear sunfish grinds up snail shells with a special set of teeth in its throat.

Although snails make up a large part of its diet, the redear also eats insect larvae and other typical sunfish foods. Redears feed mostly on bottom, but occasionally grab food on the surface. They seldom feed in water colder than 45°F.

Like bluegills, redears prefer clear water with moderately dense weeds. Stumps, roots and logs are favorite hangouts. They prefer more shade and live in deeper water than most other sunfish, sometimes moving to depths of 25 to 35 feet during summer.

Native to the Southeast, redears have been stocked in a few southwestern and northwestern states. They favor large lakes and reservoirs, but can be found in smaller lakes, ponds and slow-moving streams. They can live in slightly brackish water.

Adult redears have a bright red or orange margin around the ear flap. The colored border is wider on males than it is on females. The back and sides are light olive-green to gold; the breast yellow to yellow-orange. Redears resemble pumpkinseeds, but they do not have wavy blue cheek lines.

Redears produce fewer young than other sunfish, so they are less likely to overpopulate a lake and become stunted. They grow more quickly and reach larger sizes than bluegills in the same body of water. Most redears are 7 to 10 inches long. The world record was caught in a Virginia farm pond in 1970. It weighed 4 pounds, 8 ounces.

Redear Sunfish Range

Pumpkinseeds

Pumpkinseeds do not grow as large as bluegills or redears, but their stunning colors and willingness to bite make them a favorite among many anglers.

Originally a fish of the north central and eastern United States, pumpkinseeds have been stocked in many parts of the West. They prefer slightly cooler waters than other sunfish. Pumpkinseeds often thrive in small, shallow lakes, sheltered bays on larger lakes, or quiet areas of slow-moving streams. They seldom venture into expanses of open water. Pumpkinseeds inhabit shallower water and denser vegetation than bluegills and redears. They are not found in brackish water.

The sides of a pumpkinseed are mostly gold with green, orange and red flecks, and iridescent blue and emerald reflections. The underside is bronze to red-orange. Wavy blue lines mark the side of the head. The ear flap has a half-moon spot of bright red at the tip. Females have the same markings as males, but their colors are not quite as intense.

Insects make up the bulk of the pumpkinseed's diet, but it eats many other foods, including snails and small baitfish. Pumpkinseeds have smaller mouths than most other sunfish, which explains their habit of nibbling at baits.

Pumpkinseeds will take food on the surface or on bottom. They feed heavily during the spawning period and into early summer. Feeding slows in mid-summer, but picks up again in fall.

Often called *common sunfish,* pumpkinseeds usually reach 5 to 7 inches in length. An 8-inch or ½-pound fish is considered a good catch. The world-record pumpkinseed, 12½ ounces, was caught in Lake Carthage, South Dakota in 1970.

Pumpkinseed Range

Redbreast Sunfish

Redbreasts are at home in current or still water. Look for them in deep, slow stretches of clear, rocky streams, especially where there is vegetation. They will not hold in fast current. In lakes, they prefer deep, weedy areas with sand or mud bottoms. Like redears, redbreasts can live in slightly brackish water.

Native to the Atlantic Coast states and as far north as New Brunswick, redbreasts have been stocked in many southern states.

The redbreast, or *yellowbelly*, is named for its orange-red to yellow breast. Blue streaks and pale red spots mark its golden-brown sides. Its long, black ear flap does not have a light-colored margin.

The average size of an adult redbreast is only 6 inches or about 4 ounces. But they sometimes grow much larger. The world-record redbreast weighed 2 pounds. It was caught in the Lumber River, South Carolina in 1975.

Redbreasts are more prone to feed at night than other sunfish. Primarily bottom feeders, they will also take food on the surface. Their diet is similar to that of other sunfish.

Although they form loose schools most of the year, redbreasts begin to congregate in dense schools in deep water once the temperature drops below 40°F. Fish in these schools seldom bite and almost seem to be hibernating.

Redbreast Sunfish Range

Warmouth

Swamps, sloughs, backwaters and weedy bays of lakes provide homes for warmouth. They can survive in water too stagnant for most other sunfish. Warmouth prefer warm, shallow areas with dense brush, logs, weeds or other thick cover. They can live in slightly brackish water, but cannot tolerate a salt content as high as redears or redbreasts.

Warmouth thrive in the southeastern United States. But their low reproductive rate prevents them from becoming as numerous as other sunfish. Their native range extends as far north as central Wisconsin and as far west as Texas. They have been stocked in waters west of the Rocky Mountains.

The warmouth is often confused with the rock bass (page 122). Both species have reddish eyes, large mouths and olive-brown sides with brown mottling. But the warmouth only has three spines in the anal fin compared to six on the rock bass. The warmouth also has several reddish-brown streaks that radiate from the eye and extend across the head.

During summer, warmouth feed heavily in early morning. Feeding slows by late afternoon. Adults prefer insects and small crayfish, although they eat many other sunfish foods.

Warmouth average 7 to 8 inches in length; a large one measures 10 inches. The world record, 2 pounds, 2 ounces, was caught in Douglas Swamp, South Carolina in 1973.

Warmouth Range

Green Sunfish

The green sunfish has a large mouth and a long body that closely resembles a bass. Its brown to olive-green sides are tinged with emerald green, and the undersides are white or yellow.

These hardy sunfish will tolerate conditions too harsh for most other sunfish. They can survive murky water, low oxygen levels and fluctuating temperatures and water levels. However, they are not found in brackish water. They prefer heavy cover such as large rocks, brush piles or dense weeds.

Green sunfish average only 5 to 6 inches, but two fish, each weighing 2 pounds, 2 ounces, have been recorded. One was caught in a Kansas strip mine in 1961; the other in Stockton Lake, Missouri in 1971. Because of its large mouth, the green sunfish can eat foods like crayfish, shad, young crappies and even small carp. Green sunfish feed most heavily at dawn and dusk.

Green Sunfish Range

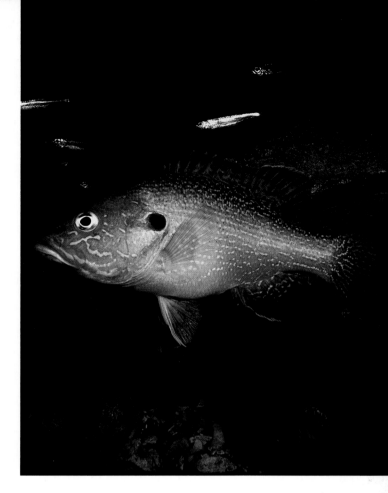

Longear Sunfish

Longears are small but colorful, averaging only 4 to 5 inches in length. The largest longear on record, 14¾ ounces, was caught in Elephant Butte Reservoir, New Mexico in 1979.

Orange and turquoise mottle the longear's sides and wavy blue lines cross the cheeks. The back is olive-green to rust-brown, and the breast is pale red, orange or yellow. Like the green sunfish, the longear has a black ear flap with a red or yellow margin. But the longear's gill flap is much longer than that of the green sunfish.

Longears prefer slack-water areas of clear streams, but they also inhabit lakes, reservoirs, estuaries and ponds. They usually live in shallow, weedy areas, but do not require heavy cover. Because of their small size, longears eat tiny foods, particularly insects. They often take food on the surface, and may feed at night.

Longear Sunfish Range

Where to Find Sunfish

If you can find sunfish, chances are you can catch them. Sunfish in natural lakes and reservoirs move more than many anglers realize. They change location depending on the season and daily weather patterns, so experts adjust their fishing strategies accordingly. Sunfish in streams, ponds, canals and other small waters do not move as much from one season to the next, so fishermen have less trouble finding them.

NATURAL LAKES. Early in the season, angling remains slow until the water warms to about 60°F. Fishermen willing to work hard for a few sunfish can find them in shallow, mud-bottomed bays. These bays are the first to offer new weed growth and a supply of insects and other small foods.

Fishing improves as spawning time approaches. Sunfish hang in water slightly deeper than their spawning grounds. They move into the nesting area on a warm day, but move out again when the weather cools.

Spawning sunfish prefer shallow, protected bays. If none are available, they will spawn along a sheltered shoreline. Most fish nest on firm sand or gravel bottoms. They rarely spawn over soft mud. Sunfish prefer emergent vegetation, but will nest around submerged weeds if emergents are not available. They nest within loosely-spaced vegetation. In dense weeds, look for them along edges or in pockets. After spawning, sunfish drift back to their pre-spawn locations. Some fish return to the shallows to

Sunfish Locations in Natural Lakes

SPAWNING AREAS for sunfish in natural lakes include: (1) shallow bays with sand or gravel bottoms, (2) sheltered shorelines, (3) points with stands of emergent weeds, (4) sandy beach, (5) boat harbor.

SUMMER locations include: (1) weedlines along drop-offs, (2) submerged extensions of shoreline points, (3) mid-lake ridge or hump, (4) gradually tapering points, (5) docks and boathouses in deep water.

spawn again a week or two later. Others move to summer locations.

Big bluegills and shellcrackers spend most of the summer just outside weedlines. They concentrate near areas where the weedline forms points, notches and inside turns. In a clear lake, they may spend the summer at depths exceeding 20 feet. Pumpkinseeds do not move quite as deep. Small bluegills and shellcrackers, and the smaller sunfish species like longears and greens, remain in the shallows through summer. Sunfish will suspend to feed on plankton, especially on calm, sunny days. The fish often hang just off a weedline, but may suspend in deep, open areas.

As the surface temperature begins to drop in early fall, large sunfish return to shallower water in bays and along breaklines, especially those close to shore. They remain in these areas until the surface water cools to the same temperature as deep water. But as the lake begins to turn over, the fish scatter and become difficult to find. In the North, most anglers stop fishing until freeze-up.

Surface temperatures of lakes in the Deep South range from 50° to 60°F during winter. Fishermen continue to catch sunfish in deep fringes of emergent weeds and in mid-lake holes with weedy or brushy cover.

RESERVOIRS. The same principles govern sunfish movement in lakes and reservoirs, although the types of habitat may differ. Most fish move into the back ends of creek arms, or coves, to spawn. The best coves are at least 20 feet deep at the entrance to

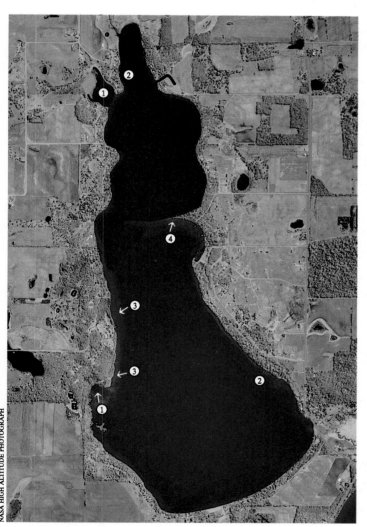

EARLY FALL locations include; (1) shallow bays with submerged vegetation, (2) docks and boathouses in shallow water, (3) shallow shoals with submerged weeds, (4) shallow submerged weedbed off shoreline point.

LATE FALL-WINTER locations include: (1) deep water off sharp drop-offs, (2) deep water off shoreline points, (3) inside turns of shoreline breaks, (4) deep holes, (5) deep bays.

the main lake. Shallower coves generally attract only small fish. Sunfish prefer creek arms with clear, inflowing streams. Avoid coves fed by muddy creeks, because the bottom will probably be too soft for sunfish to nest.

Most sunfish spawn on gradually-sloping sand or gravel points, especially those exposed to the sun. But they will spawn on shallow flats adjacent to the creek channel or along straight shorelines. The best spawning areas have some weeds, brush, timber or stumps for cover.

Prior to spawning, sunfish hold in water at least 10 feet deep. Look for them in creek channels or in deep water off points. Like sunfish in lakes, they move into the shallows on warm days and out on cold days.

After spawning, sunfish scatter in deeper water. But some fish remain near the nest areas and return to spawn a second or even a third time. Each successive spawn takes place in deeper water.

Some sunfish remain in deep coves all summer. But if a cove is less than 10 feet deep, sunfish will usually move to the main body of the reservoir. To locate fish, you must find structure with weeds, brush or trees that provide shelter in the shallows. The structure must also be near deep water, because big sunfish will retreat as deep as 30 feet during extremely hot weather.

Prime summertime structure includes creek and river channels, points and flats. Look for edges where channels slope into deep water. Sunfish prefer outside bends and intersections with other channels.

Sunfish Locations in Reservoirs

SPAWNING AREAS include: (1) back ends of both creek arms and secondary creek arms, (2) gradually-sloping points, (3) flats near the creek channel (small dashes), (4) shallow humps, (5) wooded main lake coves.

SUMMER locations include: (1) edge of creek channel, (2) edge of river channel (large dashes), (3) channel intersection, (4) deep points in creek arm, (5) submerged points in main lake, (6) sunken island in main lake.

Select main lake points that slope gradually into deep water. Look for flats that top out at 10 to 20 feet. Sunfish congregate in depressions on the flats. Man-made features like fish attractors and docks also hold sunfish in summer.

Sunfish in reservoirs, like those in natural lakes, will suspend in open water. Anglers find them feeding on plankton or insects over deep water.

In early fall, sunfish move back to their pre-spawn locations. They hang along breaklines adjacent to areas where they spawned in spring, but move shallower on warm days. But they do not go as shallow as they did at spawning time. Sunfish remain in these areas and continue to bite until the surface temperature drops to about 60°F. Then, they begin moving to deep wintering grounds.

In southern waters, few anglers pursue sunfish during the winter months. Fishermen catch some fish along sharp-breaking structure, usually at depths of 25 to 40 feet. The fish may move shallower after several warm, sunny days.

DAILY MOVEMENT. Weather and changing light levels affect daily movements of sunfish. Like almost all freshwater fish, they avoid bright sunlight. But they seem less sensitive to light than most other fish. They retreat to slightly deeper water on bright days, but do not move as deep as many other species. Most types of sunfish seek shade to escape the sun, but do not need dense cover.

Cold fronts affect sunfish much like other species. The fish move to deeper water and refuse to bite until a day or two after the front passes.

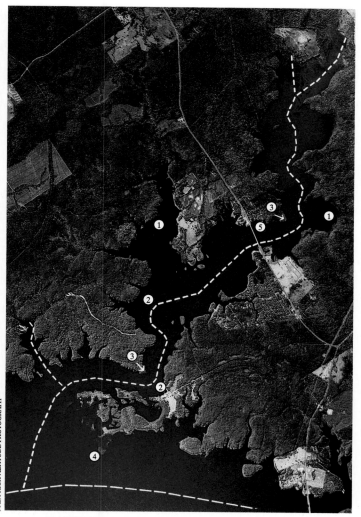

EARLY FALL locations include: (1) brushy shorelines, (2) outside bends of the creek channel, (3) shallow points near the creek channel, (4) shallow points in the main lake, (5) docks and marinas close to deep water.

LATE FALL-WINTER locations include: (1) creek channel-river channel intersection, (2) deep water in river channel, (3) deep main lake coves, (4) steep main lake points, (5) deep water at lower end of creek arm.

Fishing for Sunfish

Catching small sunfish is easy. But taking big ones requires more know-how. Small sunfish form large, loose schools near the shelter of shallow weeds, docks, bridges or other cover in shallow water. Even inexperienced fishermen have little trouble finding them. In addition, small sunnies are curious, often swarming around any small object tossed into their midst.

Bigger sunfish tend to be loners, but occasionally collect in small groups. They stay in deeper water and are less inquisitive than small sunfish. They inspect baits carefully, backing off from anything that looks suspicious.

To present a bait or lure naturally, expert panfish anglers use light line and small hooks. Six-pound, clear monofilament works well in most situations. But some fishermen prefer 4-pound line in extremely clear water or when the fish seem reluctant to bite. In timber, brush or dense weeds, many use line as heavy as 20-pound test to free snagged hooks.

Most sunfish have tiny mouths, so #8 or #10 hooks are good choices. Some anglers use even smaller hooks when fishing with insect larvae. A #6 may work better for large sunfish or for species with large mouths, like warmouth and green sunfish.

Sunfish often swallow the bait. Some fishermen prefer long-shank hooks, so they can remove them quickly. But hooking fish is easier with a short-shank hook. You can remove the shorter hook with a disgorger or a longnose pliers.

A sunfish usually swims up to a bait, studies it for an instant, then inhales it by sucking in water which is expelled out the gills. But a sunfish may spit the bait just as quickly, especially if it feels the hook. To avoid this problem, some fishermen cover the point with bait. Normally, you should wait a few seconds before setting the hook. But when the fish are fussy, set the hook at the first sign of a bite.

When you hook a sunfish, it instinctively turns its body at a right angle to the pressure. Water resistance against the fish's broad, flat side makes it difficult to gain line. This trait makes sunfish one of the toughest fighting panfish.

You can catch sunfish with a wide variety of techniques. Most fishermen simply dangle live bait from a small bobber. But fly-fishing, casting small lures, and even slow-trolling or drifting in deep water often produce good catches.

If an area holds sunfish, they will usually bite within a few minutes after you begin fishing, or they will not bite at all. It seldom pays to wait them out. The best sunfish anglers spend only 5 to 10 minutes in a spot if they are not catching fish.

Many panfish anglers make the mistake of using heavy rods, big hooks or large floats. Some even attach thick steel leaders. Although sunfish are strong fighters, you do not need heavy-duty equipment to land them. Heavy tackle reduces the number of bites and detracts from the sport of fighting these scrappy fish.

Lures for Sunfish

LURES include: (1) popper, (2) Timberwolf, (3) Western Bee, (4) Emmy Jig with mealworm, (5) rubber spider, (6) Creme Angle Worm, (7) Beetle Spin™, (8) Devil Spinner, (9) Panther Martin, (10) Black Fury® Combo, (11) Hal-Fly®, (12) Road Runner®, (13) Sassy® Shad, (14) Jiggly.

Many sunfish anglers prefer artificial lures. Artificials eliminate the problems of buying and keeping live bait, especially when fishing in remote areas. And at certain times, lures are more productive.

Artificial lures work best in summer when the fish are most active. When you locate a concentration of active sunfish, artificials may outfish live bait because you do not waste time baiting the hook.

Many consider fly-fishing with surface lures to be the ultimate in panfish sport. Fly-fishing is most effective on warm summer evenings, at spawning time, or during an insect hatch. Surface-feeding sunfish will strike a popper, but may ignore live bait.

Sunfish prefer small lures. A big bluegill may strike a 6-inch plastic worm intended for bass, but an inch-long lure will catch sunfish more consistently. Always retrieve the lure slowly. Sunfish seldom strike fast-moving lures or those that produce too much noise or flash.

Anglers can make their own artificials or modify lures such as plastic worms and spinnerbaits to make them more effective.

Tips for Making Lures More Effective

SLICE a plastic worm into thin, 1- to 1½-inch strips. The small pieces can be easily inhaled by sunfish. Trim excess hair from a jig or popper to tempt more strikes and catch more fish.

CHANGE spinner blades or jig bodies on a spinnerbait to alter the color or action. Many anglers buy plain spinnerbait arms, then add blades and jig bodies to suit the conditions.

Natural Bait for Sunfish

Sunfish rely heavily on scent to find food, so it is not surprising that the vast majority of sunfish are caught on natural bait.

Natural bait works best early and late in the year when the water is too cold for sunfish to chase artificial lures. It is also the best choice for fishing deep or murky water. When a cold front slows fishing, sunfish may refuse artificials but continue to bite on natural bait.

Small baits like waxworms, red wigglers and mayfly nymphs usually work best in spring and fall. Larger baits like grasshoppers, crickets, catalpa worms, nightcrawlers and cockroaches may work better during summer when sunfish feed more actively.

Sunfish prefer a bait that squirms enticingly on the hook. When using worms, for example, let the ends dangle. To keep your bait alive as long as possible, use light-wire hooks because they do the least damage to the bait.

Some anglers chum with worms or bits of fish, clams or shrimp to draw sunfish into an area. Check local regulations before using this technique.

BAITS include: (1) cricket, (2) grasshopper, (3) piece of nightcrawler, (4) garden worm, (5) red wiggler, (6) small leech, (7) minnow, (8) grass shrimp, (9) clam meat, (10) waxworm, (11) mealworm. Hook sizes range from a #10 with a cricket to a #6 with a garden worm.

Tips for Using Natural Bait

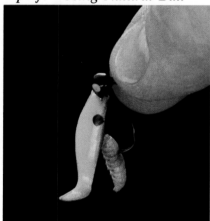

ADD natural bait to an artificial to make the lure more appealing. Sunfish will hold the lure an instant longer before spitting it.

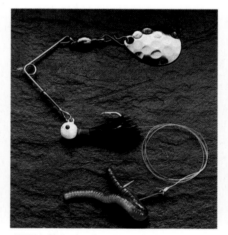

ATTACH a trailer hook with live bait behind an artificial lure, such as a small spinnerbait. The lure attracts sunfish to the bait.

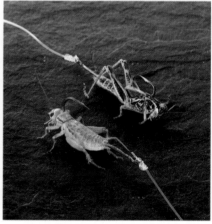

THREAD crickets and grasshoppers on long-shank, light-wire hooks. The point should protrude between the collar and head, or pierce the collar.

Fishing for Spawning Sunfish

Spawning time offers the fastest sunfish action of the year. The fish concentrate in shallow areas where fishermen can easily find them. Nest-guarding males attack baits or lures that come too close, and females feed through the spawning period.

Your chances of finding heavy concentrations of fish are best early in the spawning season. Sometimes individual fish will nest several times over the course of the summer. Many experts believe that sunfish spawn only within a few days of a full or new moon.

In murky waters, sunfish may nest as shallow as 6 inches. But in clear lakes, anglers sometimes catch spawning sunfish in water 15 feet deep. Big sunfish usually nest deeper than small ones.

Sunfish often return to the same spawning grounds year after year. The same fish may spawn several times over the course of the season. Once you find a spawning area, carefully note its location so you can find it again. Many southern fishermen claim they can locate spawning sunfish by smell. The fish, especially bluegills and redears, emit a musky, fish-like odor.

You can prolong your fishing by moving to new waters as the spawning season progresses. Sunfish nest earliest in shallow, murky lakes because they warm the fastest. When they complete spawning in these waters, others are just beginning in deep, clear lakes. Sunfish spawn earlier in the South than in the North. In Florida, bluegills begin spawning in February compared to May and June in Wisconsin.

Avoid spooking fish when you approach beds in shallow water. Move slowly, keep a low profile and do not make unnecessary noise. Cast beyond, then retrieve your lure or bait into the nest area.

Some anglers motor slowly through likely spawning areas, then mark the nests by poking sticks into the bottom or tossing out small styrofoam markers. The activity may spook the fish, but they usually return within 15 minutes. Fishermen then sneak back to work the nests.

When fishing for spawners, set the hook the instant you feel a bite. Males instinctively grab any object that invades the nest, then carry it away. If you wait for the fish to swallow the bait, it may be too late.

Where to Find Spawning Sunfish

STUMP FIELDS in shallow water provide extra cover. A stump protects one side of the nest, making it easier for the male to guard the young.

OVERHANGING COVER, like willow branches, offers protection from birds and other predators. But sunfish will not nest in heavy shade.

EMERGENT PLANTS provide prime spawning cover. Look for fish in pockets or along the edges of bulrushes, buttonbush and cattails.

Tips for Finding Spawning Sunfish

POLE slowly through a likely spawning area or use an electric trolling motor. Look for round, light-colored depressions on bottom.

LOOK for ripples, wakes or other surface disturbances that reveal the location of spawners. Keep the sun at your back for best visibility.

MOVE SLOWLY along the edge of emergent weeds, while casting toward the vegetation. Or fan-cast a potential spawning area to locate fish.

How to Use a Bobber Rig for Spawning Sunfish

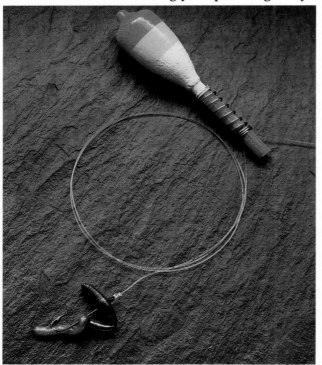

ATTACH a small float to 6-pound monofilament and tie on a #8 light-wire hook. Do not use a sinker. Bait with a small worm or cricket.

LOB the rig beyond the spawning bed to prevent spooking the fish. Reel slowly, then stop when the float is directly above the nest.

How to Fly-cast for Spawning Sunfish

FLY LURES include: (1) Black Gnat, (2) rubber spider, (3) Wooly Worm, (4) Royal Coachman, (5) Miller, (6) popper, (7) McGinty, (8) Mosquito, (9) Light Cahill.

MULTIPLE EXPOSURE PHOTOGRAPH

PAUSE a few seconds while your bug or fly sinks. Twitch the line, then pause again. To detect a strike, watch for a slight tug where the line enters the water.

KEEP the bait 6 to 12 inches off bottom. Twitch the bobber periodically so the bait rises a few inches, then settles toward bottom. If this technique fails to catch fish, remove the bobber, attach a small split-shot, and drag the bait slowly along bottom. Sunfish will attack any bait that comes too close to the nest.

TWITCH a surface lure gently, then wait for the ripples to die. Avoid twitching it too hard because the sudden motion may spook the fish.

SET the hook immediately when a sunfish strikes. Sometimes a fish will make a swirl or splash as it grabs the lure. Or it may suck in the lure with barely a ripple.

STUMPS, especially large ones, provide excellent cover. Wave action washes soil away from the roots, creating open spaces where sunfish can hide.

Fishing for Sunfish in Trees and Brush

Submerged trees or brush provide prime sunfish habitat in almost every type of fresh water. In spring, sunfish spawn in or near timber and brush in shallow water. Later in the year, they find cover and food around trees and brush in deeper water.

All types of sunfish relate to timber and brush, but these cover types are especially attractive to bluegills, redears and warmouth.

Any woody cover will hold sunfish. But some trees hold more fish than others. Cedars and oaks, for example, offer excellent cover. They have a dense network of branches and they rot more slowly than most other trees.

When scouting for sunfish, look for trees that indicate bottom type. Pine trees, for instance, grow mainly on sandy soil, so they may reveal the locations of spawning areas.

Trees and brush near some type of structure generally hold more sunfish than a flat expanse with similar cover. For example, a fallen tree on a point will usually attract more sunfish than a fallen tree along a straight shoreline with uniform depth. A change in the height of trees often provides a clue to bottom structure. A stand of trees growing higher than the surrounding timber may pinpoint the location of a drop-off.

Snags pose a constant problem when fishing in timber and brush. To offset this problem, try the following strategies. Rig your rod and reel with 12- to 15-pound line and a heavy sinker. The extra weight enables you to bounce the sinker to free a snagged lure. Or use 4-pound mono and a tiny lure like a $\frac{1}{32}$-ounce jig. Cast over submerged brush or tree limbs, then retrieve slowly, allowing the jig to occasionally bump the branches. If you snag a branch, do not shake it violently while trying to free the lure. This will scare the fish away. Instead, break the line, tie on a new hook and resume fishing.

FLOODED TIMBER near the banks of shallow coves often holds sunfish in spring. In summer, look for trees along a creek channel or near the entrance to a cove.

FALLEN TREES near deep water usually hold sunfish, especially if they have a lot of branches. Some anglers cut down trees to make hiding spots for sunfish.

OVERHANGING LIMBS offer shade and a source of food. Insects collect on the limbs and fall into the water, where they are eaten by sunfish.

SHALLOW BRUSH provides cover in early season and during periods of high water. Sunfish use deeper brush patches in summer.

How to Fish Submerged Limbs

REACH into openings with a long pole. A heavy sinker supported by a large bobber helps avoid snags.

SLIDE a clip-on sinker down the line if you become snagged. The impact will usually free the hook.

USE a light-wire hook and strong line in thick brush. If you snag a limb, pull hard to straighten the hook.

How to Fish Standing Timber

CAST beyond a large submerged tree, then let the line flow from the spool as the lure or bait sinks to bottom. Retrieve as close to the tree as possible.

DROP your bait or lure straight down alongside a tree. If the tree has branches protruding at different depths, cover them all thoroughly.

How to Fish a Stump

MOVE your rod tip to the side as you retrieve so the bait hits a stump. Sunfish usually ignore a bait more than a foot away from their hiding place.

COVER the edge of a stump by circling it with a long pole. Sunfish hide among the roots, so you must place your bait close to the stump.

How to Fish a Fallen Tree

CLIMB out onto the trunk of a fallen tree. Or tie your boat to a limb, or anchor off to one side and cast toward the tree. In early season, concentrate on shallow water near shore. When the water warms, fish the submerged branches in deeper water. If fishing a stream, work the slack water downstream of the tree.

How to Fish Overhanging Limbs

POSITION your boat to the side of overhanging limbs and fly-cast a surface lure under the branches. Fly-casting works well in this situation, because sunfish are accustomed to feeding on insects that drop into the water. Or you can flip a bait into the opening with a flippin' rod or any type of long pole.

How to Fish Shoreline Brush

MOVE along shore, dropping your bait into openings in the brush. Sunfish often hang in pockets on the inshore side of brushy cover.

POKE your bait under shoreline brush by using a long pole with only 6 to 12 inches of line at the tip. Keep the bait as close to the bank as possible.

MATTED WEEDS, or *slop,* block out sunlight. Sunfish find shade and cooler temperatures below the dense layer of vegetation. Slop usually consists of lily pads mixed with coontail or milfoil, and some type of filamentous algae. In the South, water hyacinth forms dense mats that cover entire lakes.

Fishing for Sunfish in Weeds

Weeds are prime sunfish habitat. Small sunfish hide among the leaves to escape predators. Larger fish seek the shade of overhead vegetation. Sunfish also feed on aquatic insects attracted to the weeds.

The best sunfish waters have light to moderate weed growth. If a lake has dense weeds throughout, too many sunfish survive so they become stunted.

Aquatic plants with large, wide leaves offer better cover than weeds with sparse, thin leaves. Look for sunfish in shallow weedbeds in spring. Small fish often remain in weedy shallows all summer, but larger fish prefer weeds close to deep water.

The biggest sunfish usually hang along the edges of weedbeds. Weedlines form where the water becomes too deep for plants to get enough sunlight, or where the bottom changes to a different material.

Like trees, aquatic weeds provide a clue to sunfish location by indicating the bottom type. Bulrushes, for example, grow mainly on sandy bottoms, while lily pads grow in mud. A fisherman searching for spawning sunfish would have better luck near a bulrush bed, because most species of sunfish prefer to nest on a hard bottom.

To catch sunfish in weeds, most fishermen use a light rod, a small bobber and live bait. Some prefer a long pole to reach small pockets and to lift fish straight up before they can tangle the line around plant stems. Accomplished fly-fishermen can place a popper or bug in a tiny opening by casting from a distance.

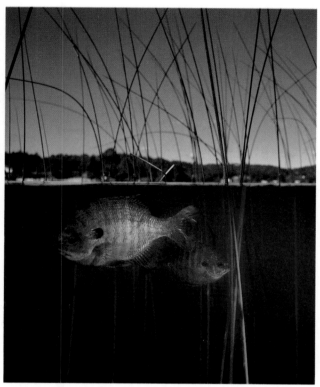

EMERGENT WEEDS like bulrushes, pickerelweed and maidencane provide spawning habitat. Some fish continue to use deep emergent weeds during summer.

FLOATING-LEAVED WEEDS such as lily pads offer early season cover as the leaves grow toward the surface. In summer, look for sunfish in lily pads near drop-offs.

SUBMERGED WEEDS, especially large-leaved pondweed, or *cabbage,* provide good summer habitat. Look for tiny flowering spikes protruding above the surface.

SAND GRASSES often form low-growing mats on large shallow flats. Look for sunfish in open holes, especially in fall. Many sand grasses have a musky odor.

IRREGULARITIES along beds of emergent weeds usually hold the most sunfish. Look for points and notches. Then cast your lure or bait close to the weeds, let it sink straight down and retrieve slowly. Sunfish hang near the base of the weeds and refuse to chase the bait or lure into open water.

STRAIGHT EDGES usually have some sunfish, but they may be scattered. To cover the edge most efficiently, stay close to the weeds and cast parallel to them.

INSIDE EDGES sometimes hold more sunfish than outside margins because they are sheltered from the wind. Look for deep areas along the inside of the weeds.

BOAT LANES cleared through emergent vegetation provide access to lakeshore cabins. Sunfish concentrate along edges of the boat lanes. Work each edge by casting parallel.

POCKETS in emergent vegetation are prime sunfish spots. In summer, look for pockets in deep water. To avoid snagging the surrounding weeds, drop the bait into the exact spot.

How to Fish Floating-leaved Weeds

LOOK for shaking lily pads to locate sunfish. The fish bump the stems and pads to dislodge insects. Or listen for the sound of sunfish slurping bugs off the surface.

KEEP your rod tip high to slide sunfish over the pads. If the fish swims below the surface, it will wrap your line around the tough stems.

How to Fish Matted Vegetation

RIP a hole in matted vegetation with an L-shaped rod made from ¾-inch, aluminum electrical conduit. Use a cane or extension pole to drop your bait into the opening.

RUN your boat into the vegetation to spread the weeds and dislodge insects. Back out, wait several minutes for the fish to return, then drop your bait into the opening.

How to Fish Submerged Weeds

RETRIEVE a plastic bubble rig so the bait just brushes the weedtops. A filled bubble will sink at about 1 foot per second. Count down to the desired depth, then reel just fast enough to keep the bait at the right level.

REEL a small spinnerbait over the weeds. A slow retrieve works best. If the lure begins to touch the weeds, raise your rod tip and reel faster. The sudden change of action may trigger a strike.

Fishing for Sunfish on Structure

Sunfish experts know that the biggest fish are usually found where the depth drops rapidly or the bottom type suddenly changes.

Any type of structure may hold sunfish, but the best structure has ample cover like brush, trees or weeds.

In early morning and late afternoon, sunfish feed in shallows adjacent to shoreline breaks and creek channels, or on the tops of points and humps. In midday, they retreat to deeper water. During summer, bluegills may go as deep as 25 feet and redears to 35 feet. Other sunfish species seldom go deeper than 15 feet.

When you locate sunfish on structure, carefully note the depth. Chances are, others will be at the same depth. Sunfish on structure rarely hang more than a foot or two off bottom. But they sometimes move away from structure and suspend in open water.

To catch sunfish on structure, most fishermen use live bait. Crickets, grasshoppers, small nightcrawlers, leeches, and insect larvae are among the favorites. Attach split-shot about a foot above the bait, and fish it on a ⅛- or ¼-ounce slip-sinker rig. Or suspend the bait a few inches off bottom with a bobber. Some anglers tip a 1/16- or 1/32-ounce jig with live bait. You can add split-shot just ahead of the jig so it sinks faster.

SHORELINE BREAKS hold sunfish throughout the year. Look for points and inside turns along the breakline. Large sunfish sometimes spawn along shallow breaklines at depths of 5 to 8 feet.

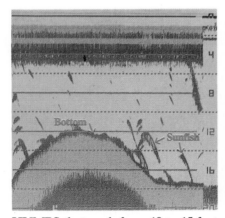

HUMPS that peak from 10 to 15 feet below the surface are good summertime spots. This graph tape shows sunfish at 11 to 15 feet alongside a hump.

POINTS attract sunfish year-round. The fish usually hold near the tip of a point or around fingers projecting off the side.

DEPRESSIONS, such as a hole in a shallow flat, draw sunfish in spring and early fall. These areas become too warm in summer.

TROLL slowly along a breakline. Zig-zag into deeper and shallower water to locate fish. Some fishermen back-troll to reduce the boat's speed. Point the stern into the wind and run the motor in reverse.

WORK the edge of a creek channel by motoring slowly within easy casting distance of the timber. Cast into the shallows, then retrieve the bait or lure down the slope, keeping it close to bottom.

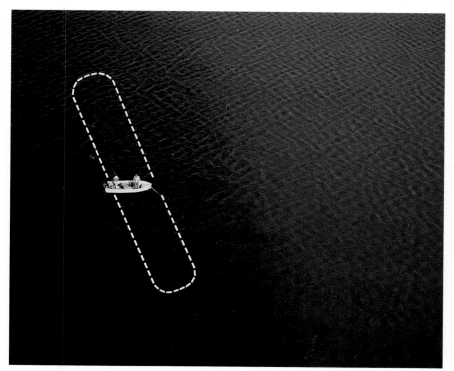

ANCHOR the boat when you locate sunfish. To work a drop-off efficiently, place one anchor in the shallows and another in deep water (page 16). Then cast parallel to the breakline at the depth you found fish. From this position, you can cover all the area within the dotted lines.

AVOID anchoring in deep water, then casting into the shallows. Your lure or bait will pass through the strike zone (circle) for only an instant.

ANCHORED BOATS, rafts and other floating objects may provide the only shade in areas that have flat, barren bottoms. Sunfish will form loose schools just below a boat that has been moored for several days.

Fishing for Sunfish Around Man-made Features

In lakes that lack natural cover and structure, man-made features are excellent sunfish spots. Docks, piers, boathouses, duck blinds and swimming platforms offer shade and overhead cover. Other features like bridges, submerged roadbeds, riprap banks and even anchored boats hold fish. Where there is an abundance of natural sunfish habitat, man-made features attract fewer fish.

Many anglers place brush piles or other homemade attractors near docks or favorite fishing spots. An attractor can make a good spot even better.

Man-made features in the shallows draw large sunfish in spring and fall, especially if deep water is nearby. But only small fish remain when the water warms. Man-made objects in 10 to 15 feet of water will hold big fish during the summer months.

Most anglers suspend their bait near submerged man-made objects. But you need special techniques to reach sunfish under platform-like features. If the water is calm, try skipping a lure under a dock, much like you would skip a rock across the water. Or use a long pole to poke your bait under a swimming platform.

Where to Find Sunfish Around Man-made Features

BANK PROTECTORS, especially those made of corrugated metal, offer hiding spots for sunfish. The fish hold in the indentations.

FISH ATTRACTORS vary from crib shelters to bundles of brush. These crib shelters will be hauled to a desired location, then sunk with blocks.

DOCKS in water 10 to 15 feet deep with some weeds or brush nearby may draw large sunfish. But docks in shallow water attract only small fish.

How to Fish Docks and Swimming Platforms

FLICK your lure or bait under a dock with an underhand motion. Or cast sidearm so your lure hits the water in front of the dock and skips under it.

PUSH your bobber under a swimming platform, then bring your pole back out. This technique places your bait near fish in the shade of the platform.

Tips for Catching Sunfish Around Fish Attractors

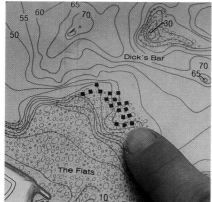

PINPOINT the location of fish attractors by referring to a lake map. Attractors (squares) placed by resource agencies are usually marked on maps.

SUSPEND your bait so it hangs just above a stakebed or other type of attractor. Some anglers prefer bobbers; others fish vertically without floats.

LINE UP two distant objects so you can find the attractor on future trips. These anglers have lined up the edge of a house with a water tower.

Tips for Fishing Other Man-made Features

WALK along the top of a bank protector. Drop your bait next to the wall, because sunfish usually hug the wall tightly. Or pull your boat close to the wall and cast parallel to it.

FLY-CAST around lighted fishing piers just after dark. Use a dry fly or tiny popper to catch sunfish rising to feed on insects attracted by the lights. Listen for slurping sounds to determine if the fish are feeding.

Fishing for Scattered Sunfish

Large sunfish lack the strong schooling instinct of smaller ones. After spawning, big sunfish, especially bluegills and redears, retreat to deeper water. Many scatter along shoreline breaks, points and humps where they remain through summer, making it difficult for anglers to catch large numbers of fish.

Most fishermen assume that sunfish hug bottom most of the time. But large sunfish often suspend during the summer months. Expert anglers sometimes catch bluegills or redears 10 feet below the surface in water 20 to 30 feet deep.

Locating scattered sunfish can be one of the toughest challenges in panfish angling. Even if you find the fish, there is no guarantee you will catch them. Sunfish have no trouble finding food in summer, so they often ignore baits or strike half-heartedly.

Be persistent as you search. Cover a lot of water and use a depth finder to zero in on the fish. You may be able to concentrate sunfish, especially redears, with a chum bag. If the fish refuse live bait, try a spinner or other flashy lure.

How to Cast for Suspended Sunfish

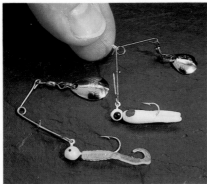

ATTACH a 1/16- or 1/32-ounce spinnerbait to 4- or 6-pound mono. Light line makes it easier to cast the tiny lure and allows it to sink deeper.

CAST the spinnerbait while drifting over open water. To locate fish, let it sink to a different depth before beginning each retrieve. Watch your depth finder closely for blips that may indicate the location of suspended sunfish. If you spot fish, work the area thoroughly before moving on.

How to Drift for Suspended Sunfish

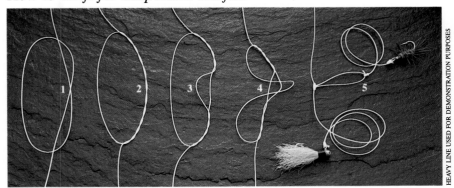

TIE a blood loop by (1) making an overhand knot where you want to form the loop. (2) Pass the free end through the overhand knot five more times. (3) Form an opening halfway between the six wraps. (4) Push the loop through the opening, then pull on both ends of the line to snug up the knot. (5) Add a short mono dropper and a wet fly. Tie a ¹⁄₁₆-ounce jig to the main line.

LOWER the rig straight down while drifting over a potential sunfish area. Experiment with different lengths of line to find the fish. If you catch a sunfish, drift through the area again.

How to Chum for Sunfish

CRUSH snails, grass shrimp or saltwater shrimp, then put them inside a cheesecloth bag. Add rocks for extra weight, then tie a long rope to the end of the bag. Some anglers toss bits of shrimp over the side of the boat.

LOWER the bag until it is on or just above bottom, then fish close by. If nothing happens in 10 minutes, move to another spot. Chum remains effective for about one hour. Add new chum when it no longer draws fish.

LOOK for mayflies clinging to leaves of willow trees or other plants along a lakeshore or streambank. Sunfish congregate below overhanging vegetation to grab insects that fall into the water. They also feed on mayfly nymphs that swim from the bottom toward the surface where they emerge as adult mayflies.

Fishing for Sunfish in Special Situations

Veteran sunfish anglers constantly watch for unusual fishing opportunities. For example, a hatch of mayflies or other aquatic insects can concentrate sunfish in the shallows and start a feeding spree. Grasshoppers or other land insects fall or are blown into the water, causing sunfish to snug up to the bank and wait for an easy meal.

Fishermen sometimes fail to recognize good sunfish spots. Heated discharges from power plants often draw sunfish during coldwater periods. Beaver ponds and piles of fresh beaver cuttings are commonly overlooked.

Many streams offer excellent fishing, especially for redbreast, green and longear sunfish. Look for slack-water areas off the main channel. Canals and drainage ditches connected to sunfish waters may hold large numbers of fish.

Ponds provide top-quality fishing in some regions, especially in central and southern states where winterkill is not a problem. Several state-record sunfish have been caught in ponds, including a 2-pound green sunfish in Illinois and a 4-pound, 3½-ounce bluegill in Kentucky.

Many ponds, however, contain only stunted sunfish. To combat this problem, some pond owners install sunfish feeders. Most of these devices dispense food pellets; others are platforms that hold the carcass of a dead animal so maggots continually fall into the water. Sunfish that learn to use these feeders grow larger than others in the pond.

How to Fish an Insect Hatch

WATCH for sunfish dimpling the surface as they pick off hatching insects. Hatches usually begin in late afternoon and continue into the night.

SELECT a fly or popper that resembles the hatching insect. You do not have to match the hatch exactly, but the fly should be about the same size as the insect.

How to Fish in Streams

CAST a jig or spinner tipped with a worm into a quiet pool and retrieve slowly near bottom. The best pools have weeds, logs or rocks.

DRIFT a lightly-weighted bait along an undercut bank. Cast close to the bank, then let the current sweep the bait under the cover.

DROP live bait on a bobber rig into the eddy just downstream of a fallen tree or log jam. Work the openings between branches.

How to Fish Other Unusual Spots

TIME your fishing to coincide with the cycle of a mechanized feeder. Sunfish learn to congregate near the device at feeding times.

WORK a beaver lodge or a pile of cuttings with a small nightcrawler rigged Texas-style on a plain hook. Imbedding the point prevents the hook from snagging.

Crappies

All About Crappies

Crappies rank near the top with panfish anglers because they are easy to catch and live in a wide variety of waters.

There are two species of crappies: black and white. Depending on the region, fishermen refer to both types as *specks, papermouths, bachelor perch, white perch, calico bass* and many other colorful names.

Crappies belong to the sunfish family. They have flat, silvery bodies with black to dark green markings. These markings vary in intensity, depending on the time of year and type of water. During the spring spawning period, a male black crappie may appear jet black over much of its body. Markings on male white crappies darken around the head, breast and back. Crappies from clear waters usually have bolder patterns than fish from murky waters.

The original range of black crappies included most of the eastern half of the United States, with the exception of New England. They have been introduced in many western states and even British Columbia. White crappies were originally found within a region extending from eastern South Dakota to New York, then south to Alabama and Texas. They have been introduced as far west as California.

Although black and white crappies share many of the same waters, black crappies are most abundant in cool, northern lakes with gravel or sand bottoms. They are almost always found around vegetation.

Both species live in rivers and streams, but black crappies prefer quieter waters. They can tolerate a higher salt content, which explains why they are more common than white crappies in estuaries along the East and Gulf coasts.

White crappies are most common in reservoirs, lakes, rivers and bayous of the South. They can tolerate murkier water than black crappies and can thrive in basins with either soft or hard bottoms. They usually live near some type of cover.

The two crappie species vary somewhat in their behavior. White crappies do not school as tightly as blacks. In waters where both kinds are found, white crappies normally spawn slightly deeper.

Black Crappie Range

Although they differ slightly in appearance, habitat and behavior, black and white crappies have many common characteristics. Both have a large number of gill rakers, which they use to strain plankton from the water. Crappies also eat small fish, insects, mollusks and crustaceans. In many southern reservoirs, they feed heavily on gizzard and threadfin shad.

More sensitive to light than sunfish, crappies feed most heavily at dawn, dusk or at night. They bite throughout the year, but feed less often once the water drops below 50°F.

Crappies spawn earlier than any other member of the sunfish family. They usually nest when the water temperature reaches 62° to 65°F, which can be as early as January in the Deep South or as late as June in the North.

Spawning crappies prefer gravel bottoms, but will nest on sand or mud if gravel is not available. They also spawn on boulders, dense mats of plant roots and shell beds. Most nest in weeds or brush, or near logs and other large objects. In streams, they often spawn beneath overhanging banks.

Males are the first to arrive on the spawning grounds and the last to leave. They establish and defend a territory, then build a nest by fanning away debris. After the female deposits her eggs, the male stays to protect the nest. The eggs hatch in three to five days, depending on water temperature.

Most crappies spawn in water 2 to 10 feet deep. But nesting fish have been seen in water from several inches to 20 feet deep. Usually, the larger the fish, the deeper it spawns. Spotting crappie nests can be difficult, because their beds are not as distinct as those of sunfish.

Crappie populations fluctuate widely in most waters. About once every three to five years, an unusually large percentage of young crappies survive. They grow slowly because so many fish compete for a limited food supply. As a result, anglers catch only small fish for two or three years. But once predation, angling pressure and natural mortality reduce the population, fishermen will enjoy a year or two of good fishing for large crappies.

White Crappie Range

In most waters, a good-sized crappie is ½ to 1 pound. Crappies seldom live longer than five years. The world-record white crappie weighed 5 pounds, 3 ounces. It was taken from Enid Dam, Mississippi in 1957. The world-record black crappie came from Seaplane Canal, Louisiana in 1969. It weighed 6 pounds.

BLACK CRAPPIES have irregular, dark blotches or speckles on their sides and seven or eight dorsal fin spines. The distance from the eye to the dorsal fin is equal to the length of the dorsal fin base.

WHITE CRAPPIES have five to ten vertical bands. Most have five or six dorsal fin spines; a few have seven. The distance from the eye to the dorsal fin is greater than the length of the dorsal fin base.

Where to Find Crappies

Crappies are nomads, roaming throughout natural lakes, reservoirs and large river systems. They sometimes ignore structure and cover. In one study on a Tennessee reservoir, crappies were recovered as far as 18 miles from the site where they were tagged.

The whereabouts of crappies depends on the season and weather. Movement patterns in natural lakes differ from those in reservoirs.

NATURAL LAKES. Crappies begin to bite shortly after ice-out or when the water warms to the mid-40s. The fish move into shallow, black-bottomed bays or channels connecting lakes. These waters warm faster than other areas and have the earliest crops of plankton.

In lakes that lack shallow bays or channels, look for crappies just outside weedlines. Finding them can be difficult because they may be scattered.

When temperatures rise to the mid-50s, crappies begin moving into the vicinity of their spawning areas. Black-bottomed bays often lack nesting habitat, so crappies move to areas with harder bottoms.

The best spawning areas have sand, gravel or rock bottoms. They have a moderate growth of submerged or emergent vegetation and are seldom deeper than 5 feet. Many crappies move into bays or

Crappie Locations in Natural Lakes

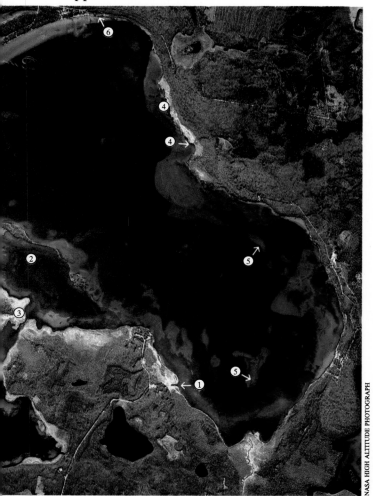

EARLY SPRING-EARLY FALL locations include: (1) dead-end channel, (2) shallow isolated bay, (3) channels connecting lakes, (4) weedy shoals, (5) shallow rock piles and sunken islands, (6) docks in shallow water.

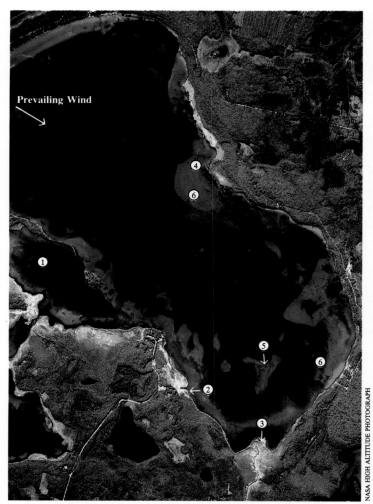

SPAWNING AREAS in natural lakes include: (1) sheltered bays, (2) dead-end channel, (3) mouth of inlet, (4) points with emergent weeds, (5) shallow humps with emergent weeds, (6) shallow flats with emergent weeds.

canals sheltered from prevailing winds, but the largest fish generally spawn on main lake shoals, points, humps and rock piles. Some crappies nest near inlets and outlets.

Crappies in bays and canals spawn earlier than fish in the main lake. Mid-lake humps warm more slowly than inshore areas and are the last to hold spawning crappies.

During the early stages of the spawning period, crappies filter into deep, sparse edges of weedbeds. At the peak of spawning, shallower, thicker parts of weedbeds hold more fish.

After spawning, crappies that nested in bays and canals return to the main lake. They often suspend just off breaklines near entrances to the bays and canals. Main lake spawners frequently scatter over a weedy flat between the spawning area and the drop-

off. In lakes without weedy flats, crappies cruise along drop-offs.

In summer, look for crappies in deeper water. Prime locations include rock piles and humps that top off at 12 to 20 feet and have some weeds.

Crappies also hang along shoreline breaks and edges of gradually tapering points. Some of the best slopes have cabbage. Although crappies usually relate to some type of structure, they may suspend over a featureless bottom.

In early fall, crappies begin moving toward the shallows. They form tight schools along weedlines or just inside them. When the weeds begin to die off, the fish school around rock piles and sunken islands in deeper water. In late fall, they move away from structure and suspend over deep water. Some fish gather near spring holes where the temperature is

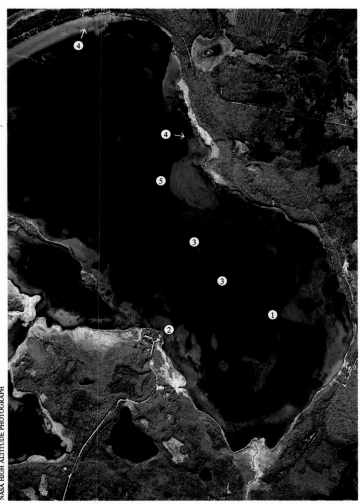

SUMMER locations include: (1) submerged point, (2) gradually tapering shoreline points, (3) deep rock piles and sunken islands, (4) irregular weedlines, (5) deep edges of weedy flats.

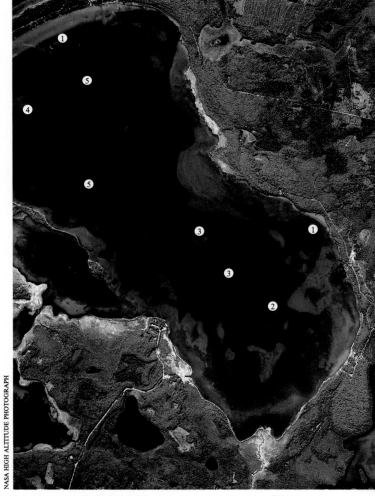

LATE FALL-WINTER locations include: (1) deep weedlines, (2) deep water off submerged point, (3) deep rock piles and sunken islands, (4) deep flats, (5) deep areas in open water.

warmer than the surrounding water. They remain in these areas through winter.

RESERVOIRS. Prior to spawning, crappies congregate around entrances to creek arms. The best arms have dense stands of timber, active streams flowing in, and maximum depths of 20 to 35 feet. As the water warms, the fish begin moving up the creek channels toward their spawning grounds. Look for them along creek channel drop-offs or in secondary coves just off the main creek arm.

Crappies usually spawn near woody cover in the back half of a cove. Check for spawning activity at the extreme back end, on shallow points, on shoreline flats or near small inlet streams. Shallow,

timbered coves off the main lake will also attract spawners. Large crappies generally nest at 3 to 4 feet; smaller fish spawn shallower.

After spawning, crappies begin filtering toward the main body of the lake. The best post-spawn locations include drop-offs along the creek channel and near standing timber, stumps, brush and fallen trees close to the channel.

Most crappies move to the main lake by summer, but some remain near creek arm entrances. Prime summertime areas also have dense, woody cover. Look for steep points near deep water, drop-offs along the main river channel, and plunging shorelines near the dam.

Crappie Locations in Reservoirs

EARLY SPRING-EARLY FALL locations include: (1) points at mouths of creek arms, (2) edges of creek channel (small dashes), (3) secondary creek arms, (4) marinas, (5) bridges, (6) shallow main lake cove.

SPAWNING AREAS include: (1) woody shallows in the back ends of coves, (2) stream inlets, (3) shallow points, (4) large flats. Some fish spawn in (5) shallow coves on the main lake.

In early fall, crappies return to the entrances of creek arms. When the water temperature drops to the mid-60s, the fish begin moving up the creek arms toward pre-spawn locations. They feed heavily along the way.

When the water falls into the mid-40s, the fish start moving back toward the main lake, stopping at post-spawn locations along the way. As winter approaches, crappies migrate to deep water near their summer haunts. They form tight schools at depths of 20 to 40 feet. Some move to depths exceeding 60 feet, but these fish are seldom caught.

DAILY MOVEMENT. Crappies usually head deeper in response to bright light. Anglers catch most fish in morning and evening, and on overcast days when fish are in shallow water. In late fall, winter and early spring, crappies frequently move into the shallows in mid-afternoon. They feed heavily once the sun has warmed the water.

Crappies commonly suspend during midday, but may suspend at any time. On dark days, they sometimes move to within a few feet of the surface.

Cold fronts have a dramatic effect on daily movement, especially before spawning. If the temperature drops in a shallow bay, crappies move to deeper water. They feed very little under cold front conditions, but fishermen who locate a concentration usually catch a few fish.

SUMMER locations include: (1) edges of main river channel (large dashes), (2) edges of creek channel, (3) intersection of main channel and creek channel, (4) submerged points in the main body of the reservoir.

LATE FALL-WINTER locations include: (1) the main river channel, (2) deep sections of the creek channel, (3) sharp-breaking shorelines, (4) deep shoreline points on the main lake, (5) deep coves on the main lake.

Fishing for Crappies

Catching crappies can be ridiculously easy; or it can be next to impossible. In spring, when crappies school in shallow bays, youngsters with cane poles take home heavy stringers. But when the fish suspend in open water, even expert anglers have trouble catching them.

Unlike sunfish which are naturally curious, crappies shy away from any unusual disturbance, especially in clear water. Even experienced scuba divers can seldom approach crappies. This fact has a bearing on your angling techniques. Keep your distance, avoid unnecessary movements or noise, and use the lightest line possible for the conditions.

The standard crappie rig consists of a small float, split-shot, and a plain hook baited with a minnow. Most fishermen in the North use #4 or #6 hooks. But southern anglers often use much larger hooks.

Many southern fishermen *tightline* for crappies. They lower the bait to bottom on a tandem hook rig tied with 2/0 to 4/0 light-wire hooks and a 1-ounce sinker. With the line nearly vertical, they bounce the sinker off stumps, logs or other snaggy cover. The heavy weight allows them to feel the cover without snagging the hooks. If a hook should become snagged, a strong pull will bend the light wire enough to free the hook.

When tightlining, most anglers use bait-casting gear or medium power spinning tackle. You can get by with ultralight spinning gear and 4-pound line in snag-free water. Veteran anglers prefer cane or extension poles with 15- to 20-pound line for fishing tight spots.

Fly-fishing for crappies has not gained widespread popularity, but it can be extremely effective, particularly at spawning time. Subsurface flies take more fish than poppers or floating bugs.

Crappies strike less aggressively than most other panfish. At times, they barely move the bobber. Or the float may start to move against the wind. With an artificial lure, the only sign of a strike may be a slight sideways movement of the line.

A slow retrieve will usually catch the most crappies. They seldom strike a fast-moving lure. Keep your line tight after setting the hook. A crappie's soft mouth tears easily, so the hook can fall out if the line goes slack.

Lures and Baits for Crappies

Minnows account for the vast majority of crappies in most waters. They are so popular that bait dealers refer to any small baitfish as a crappie minnow.

Crappies prefer 1½- to 2-inch minnows, but 3-inch baitfish sometimes work better for large crappies. Fathead minnows, called *tuffies* or *mudminnows*, are a good choice because they stay alive in the bait bucket and on the hook. Shiners are difficult to keep alive, but many fishermen consider them the best crappie bait.

Because crappies frequently suspend off bottom, many anglers use tandem hook rigs (page 72) to present minnows at different depths.

When fishing is slow, smaller baits often work better than minnows. Small jigs or teardrops tipped with insect larvae have long been popular for ice fishing. But the combination works equally well for crappies in open water.

Crappies will strike almost any small lure, but tiny jigs and spinnerbaits catch the most fish. In southern crappie tournaments, more fish are taken on jigs and jig-minnow combinations than on minnows alone. Plain jigs work well in murky waters. But when fishing clear waters, most anglers tip their jigs with minnows.

HOOK a minnow through (1) the back or (2) tail when still-fishing for crappies. When casting or trolling, hook the minnow through the (3) lips or (4) eye sockets so it swims naturally.

OTHER LIVE BAITS for crappies include: (1) crappie meat, (2) gob of garden worms, (3) piece of nightcrawler, (4) leech, (5) grasshopper, (6) cricket, (7) mayfly nymph, (8) grass shrimp.

LURES for crappies include: (1) Comet®-Mino, (2) Beetle Spin™, (3) Super Shyster®, (4) Hopkins Shorty® with pork rind, (5) Kastmaster, (6) Fat Rap®, (7) Minnow/Floater, (8) streamer, (9) McGinty, (10) White Miller, (11) Twister® Teeny, (12) Crappie Slider, (13) Sassy® Shad, (14) Quiver® Jig, (15) Dart, (16) Bumblebee Jig, (17) Lightnin'™ Bug, (18) Tiny Tube™, (19) Hal-Fly®, (20) Fuzz-E-Grub®, (21) Crappie Killer, (22) No-Alibi, (23) Road Runner®, (24) Maribou Jig, (25) Whistler®, (26) bucktail jig, (27) Crappie Jig™.

Tips for Using Live Bait

ADD a stress-reducing chemical to the water to keep shiners and other sensitive baitfish alive. This works especially well during warm weather.

CUT a thin, tapered strip of meat from the belly or side of a small crappie. Tip a spinner or jig with the strip. Or you can add a piece of pork rind.

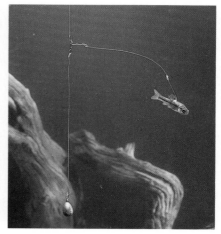

USE a tandem hook rig tied with wire spreader arms. A spreader prevents the leader from tangling with the main line or the other leader.

Fishing for Spawning Crappies

BULRUSHES offer prime spawning cover, especially in northern waters. Early in the spawning period, look for crappies along the deep edges. Later, they move into shallower parts of bulrush beds.

A stealthy approach is the key to catching spawning crappies. Even the slightest disturbance will scatter the fish off their beds. Many fishermen make the mistake of anchoring their boats in spawning areas.

To catch spawning crappies, you must place your bait near the fish, sometimes within inches. Crappies seldom leave their beds to chase food. Instead, they hover motionless near cover, waiting for baitfish to swim past. Fishermen who toss out a minnow, then wait for crappies to come to them, have little chance of success.

The depth of your bait or lure can be critical. Spawning crappies rarely feed on bottom, nor will they swim upward more than a few inches. Experiment with different depths to find the exact level.

In clear lakes, look for crappies by poling or drifting through a spawning area on a calm day. You may scare off the fish by approaching too closely, but if you mark the spot and return a few minutes later, the fish will be there.

Use light spinning gear and small minnows for spawning crappies. Suspend the baitfish below a small float, then cast beyond the spawning area and inch the bait toward the fish. Or simply dangle the minnow in front of a crappie with only a split-shot for weight.

A long pole works better than any other gear when you can see crappies. It enables you to place the bait in exactly the right spot without disturbing the fish. In southern reservoirs, fishermen use long poles to work brushy shorelines of coves. The brush is often too thick to work with standard gear, but with a long pole, you can drop your bait into small openings without getting snagged.

Fly-fishing works well for crappies spawning in light cover. Cast a minnow-like streamer beyond the fish, allow it to sink a few seconds, then retrieve slowly. Experiment to determine the right depth and whether a steady or erratic retrieve works best.

Where to Find Spawning Crappies

FLOODED BRUSH provides spawning cover in many reservoirs. Crappies also spawn in seasonally flooded brush in river backwaters.

MAIDENCANE draws spawners in waters of the Deep South. Sparse beds are the best. If fishing a thick bed, work the openings or edges.

STUMPS AND LOGS attract spawning crappies. Look for the largest stumps and those with root systems that have been washed free of soil.

How to Use a Long Pole for Spawning Crappies

MOVE quietly along the edge of a spawning area while your companion looks for crappies. Use a 12- to 14-foot extension pole with 4 to 6 feet of line at the end. Tip a jig with a small minnow hooked through the lips.

DANGLE the jig and minnow in front of the darker crappies. During the spawning period, males turn blacker than females and strike more aggressively, so your chances of catching them are greater.

How to Swim a Jig for Spawning Crappies

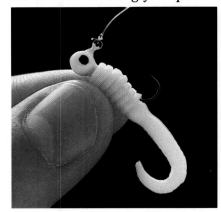

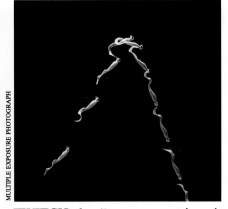

MULTIPLE EXPOSURE PHOTOGRAPH

SELECT a 1/32- or 1/64-ounce jig with a small, soft plastic tail. Some crappie fishermen attach a tiny float to keep the jig off bottom.

CAST the jig beyond the spawning area, then retrieve it slowly. Without moving the boat, fan-cast to cover the area thoroughly.

TWITCH the jig as you retrieve it over the spawning bed. As the jig slowly sinks, the curly plastic tail will wiggle enticingly.

69

FLOODED BRUSH draws crappies, especially in spring. Rising water floods scrub vegetation in reservoirs, along stream banks and in river backwaters. Deep brush piles hold crappies in summer.

Fishing for Crappies in Timber and Brush

Reservoir fishermen catch the vast majority of their crappies around various types of woody cover. Natural lakes generally have less timber and brush than reservoirs. But where anglers find such cover, they usually catch fish.

Baitfish move into timber and brush to find cover and to pick tiny organisms off the branches. Schools of crappies then move in to feed on the minnows. The cover also offers the crappies shade and protection from predators.

Shallow timber and brush provide excellent springtime cover. You can generally find crappies in water less than 6 feet deep. The wood absorbs heat from the sun and transfers it into the water, drawing fish from the surrounding area. Crappies also use this cover in fall.

During summer, crappies use woody cover in deeper water, usually 10 to 20 feet. In winter, open-water anglers catch crappies in stands of flooded timber, often as deep as 35 feet.

Most crappie fishermen use 12- to 20-pound monofilament and light-wire hooks when fishing in dense brush. Some use line as heavy as 30-pound test. Crappies do not notice the line because the branches break up its outline.

Many anglers prefer a tiny jig and a float when fishing in brushy cover where snags pose a constant problem. Adjust the float to keep the jig just above the branches, then retrieve with short twitches. The dancing jig will lure crappies out of cover.

Short casts work best in timber and brush. They enable you to place your bait or artificial lure accurately, and to control the path of your retrieve to avoid snags.

FALLEN TREES, particularly those that have toppled into deep water, are excellent spots. During midday, the fish hide among the dense branches. They may move a short distance away in morning and evening.

STUMP FIELDS attract crappies, especially if the treetops were cut off and left in the water. Stump fields near deep water hold more crappies than those on a large, shallow flat.

ROOT SYSTEMS of large trees have many crevices that offer ideal cover. Some trees have extensive lateral root systems that provide cover several feet to the side of the trunk.

STANDING TIMBER offers good crappie habitat. Crappies find cover in the treetops, among limbs and branches along the trunk and in exposed roots. Trees with bare trunks seldom hold crappies.

How to Fish Stumps and Trees

ADJUST your float so the bait rides just above an underwater stump field. Retrieve slowly or let the float drift over the stumps.

BUMP a tandem hook rig around the base of flooded trees or stumps. The heavy weight makes it easier to feel the woody cover.

JIG vertically along the shady side of a stump or standing tree. Work different depths with a lead-head jig or small jigging spoon.

How to Fish Submerged Brush

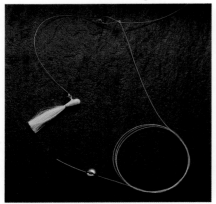

MAKE a loop in 12-pound mono 2 feet from the end. Tie on a 4-inch, 6-pound dropper and a 1/32-ounce jig. Add a split-shot heavier than the jig.

RETRIEVE so the split-shot just touches the brushtops. The shot signals contact with the brush, so you can keep the rig from constantly snagging.

PULL on the line to free the rig if you become snagged. The split-shot will slide off or the light dropper will break, leaving the rest of the rig intact.

How to Fish a Brushy Shoreline

LOOK for brush patches, standing timber, fallen trees, stumps or any other type of woody cover along a shoreline. Fish one piece of cover for a few minutes, then move on to the next. You will usually catch more crappies by covering a large area than by staying in one spot.

HOLD your boat in position with a brush clamp. This way, you do not have to drop anchor near the cover and risk spooking the fish.

DROP your bait into openings between the roots of a tree. A crappie will often hold tight in a small crevice and refuse to bite unless you dangle the bait directly in front of its nose.

WORK the stump thoroughly. Circle the entire perimeter with a long pole, but concentrate on the shady side. If the stump is hollow, try dropping your bait or lure into the center.

How to Tie a Brushguard Jig

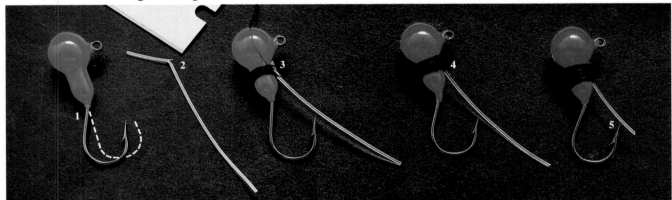

MAKE a brushguard jig by (1) bending down the shank of a small jig just behind the lead head. The dotted line shows the hook's original position. (2) With a razor blade, cut a slit in stiff, 40-pound mono. (3) Wrap winding thread around the collar several times, secure the thread in the slit, then continue wrapping. (4) Make 20 wraps, then tie off the thread with several half-hitches. (5) Trim the mono so it extends just beyond the point.

How to Free Snagged Lures

REEL in line until your rod tip touches the lure. Then push the rod to exert backward force on the lure and free the hook.

WRAP the strip-lead weight from a marker buoy around your line. With the marker cord attached, lower the weight to knock the lure free.

SLIDE a lure retriever down your line. The impact may free the lure or the chains may catch the hooks so you can pull them loose.

WEEDLINES offer excellent crappie fishing, especially at twilight or on overcast days when crappies cruise the edge of the weeds in search of food. In bright sunlight, they seek shade and cover in the weeds, but usually no more than a few feet from the edge. Weedlines provide protection from large predators as well as ambush sites where crappies can lie motionless, then dart out to grab passing baitfish.

Fishing for Crappies in Weeds

Anglers who fish natural lakes know that if they find the right kinds of weeds, they will probably find crappies. Weeds are not as important in most reservoirs, but coontail and milfoil provide good crappie cover in some man-made lakes.

In spring, crappies generally seek out some type of emergent or floating-leaved vegetation. But in summer and fall, they prefer submerged weeds. Wide-leaved varieties usually hold more crappies than narrow-leaved types. The fish prefer cabbage, but they will use narrow-leaved plants when other types are not available.

When weeds begin to die back in fall, look for crappies around plants that are still green. This vegetation offers better cover than weeds that have deteriorated. In clear lakes, you may be able to see the tops of green weeds. But in murky or deep water, you will have to snag the plants with your rod and reel.

Unlike most other panfish, crappies seldom use dense weedbeds. They prefer sparser vegetation. This allows you to use light tackle, and to retrieve jigs and other open-hooked lures without constantly snagging weeds.

WEEDTOPS often hold crappies in morning and evening, especially if there is at least 6 feet of water above the weeds. Crappies cruise through the weedtops in search of baitfish and other foods.

CLEARINGS or deep pockets in submerged weeds offer crappies an edge to which they can relate. Clearings often appear as light areas in the weeds; deep pockets look darker than the surrounding vegetation.

How to Fish a Weedline

TROLL into the wind using a jig or jig-minnow combination. When you catch a fish, mark the spot. Then work the area thoroughly, using an electric trolling motor to hold your position.

DRIFT back along the weedline, using your trolling motor to adjust the boat's direction. With the speed control set properly, the boat will drift parallel to the weedline even if the wind is blowing at an angle.

How to Fish Weedtops

SET a slip-float (page 15) so your bait rides just above the weeds. Let the float drift. A strong wind will lift the bait too far above the weeds, so you must use more weight or lower the bait by readjusting the bobber stop.

RETRIEVE a slow-sinking lure such as a spinnerbait just above the weedtops. The slower you reel, the deeper the lure will run. A 1/16- or 1/8-ounce spinnerbait works best in weeds less than 10 feet below the surface.

CAST a 1/16- or 1/8-ounce jig (1) parallel to the weedline, let it sink to bottom, then retrieve it along the edge of the weeds. Work the edge thoroughly, then (2) make a few casts into deeper water several feet out from the weeds. If these tactics fail to produce crappies, tie on a weedless lure like a Crappie Slider or a small spinnerbait. (3) Cast the lure several feet into the weeds and retrieve it slowly through the vegetation.

How to Fish in Pockets

WORK the weedtops with a plastic bubble-minnow rig. Fill the bubble with enough water so it barely sinks. Reel slowly over the weeds until you reach a deep pocket, then let the bubble and minnow settle into the hole.

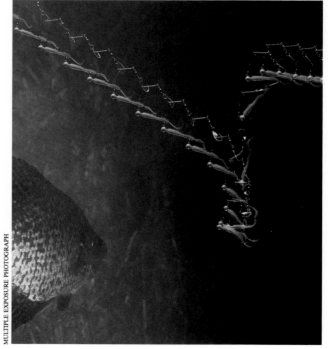

MULTIPLE EXPOSURE PHOTOGRAPH

REEL a 1/16-ounce spinnerbait into a pocket in the weeds, then pause as the lure settles. The helicopter action of the blade makes the lure sink slowly, so crappies have plenty of time to grab it.

Fishing for Crappies on Structure

ROCK PILES that top off at 12 to 20 feet hold crappies in summer. Algae on the rocks harbors tiny insect larvae that attract baitfish, which then draw crappies.

Crappies roam widely throughout most waters, using structure as underwater navigation routes. In reservoirs, for instance, crappies follow creek channels from deep water to shallow feeding areas.

Veteran crappie fishermen know which structure to fish at different times of the day and year. The upstream end of a creek channel holds few fish in midday, but often teems with crappies in the evening. A deep hump that comes alive with crappies in summer will be devoid of fish in early spring.

Many fishermen make the mistake of anchoring near structure and waiting for crappies to come to them. If they wait long enough, they may catch some fish. But you can greatly improve your odds by moving along structure until you find crappies.

Trolling with jigs works well for finding crappies on structure. Work the breakline slowly with a ⅛- or ¼-ounce jig, or use a jig-minnow combination. Lift the jig about a foot off bottom, let it sink, then repeat. Crappies usually lie in a narrow band along the breakline, so once you find the fish, you must keep the boat at the exact depth.

When you locate a school, hover over the area with an electric trolling motor. If you throw an anchor near the school, crappies will scatter.

INSIDE TURNS along a breakline hold more crappies than straight edges. Wind concentrates food in pockets formed by inside turns.

HUMPS with moderately dense weed growth on top are good summertime crappie spots. Bald humps seldom hold crappies.

POINTS with large underwater shelves protruding from the end hold more crappies than points that plunge sharply from shore.

How to Find Crappies on a Breakline

LOCATE crappies along structure with a depth finder. Crappies are easier to find than most other panfish because they usually hang farther off bottom. You can easily distinguish between the fish and the bottom signal.

PINPOINT the fish by tossing out a marker near the edge of the school. Do not throw the marker into the school. It might spook the fish and it will prevent you from working the area properly.

How to Find and Fish a Rock Pile

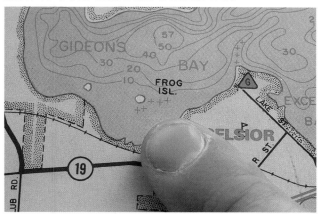

LOOK for rocky areas on your lake map. Some maps label rock reefs or indicate them by groups of closely-spaced Xs.

WATCH your depth finder for signs of a hard bottom. Rocks will return a strong signal, usually with a double or triple echo.

USE a nail instead of a sinker when snags are a problem. Tie the end of a 4-pound mono dropper around the head of a nail.

PINCH hollow, lead wire on a dropper when fishing over rocks. When snagged, the lead pulls loose so you can save the rest of the rig.

TIE on a floating jig-head to keep your bait above the rocks. The slower you retrieve, the higher the bait will ride above bottom.

Fishing for Crappies on Man-made Features

Crappies use man-made features more than any other panfish. Features like fish attractors, bridges and docks are especially important in waters that lack natural cover. In studies on two Tennessee Valley Authority reservoirs, an acre of water with artificial brush piles attracted 4.8 times more crappies than areas without the brush. And crappies in the brushy areas were substantially larger.

Features near deep water attract the most crappies. A fish attractor in water shallower than 10 feet may draw crappies in morning and evening, but seldom holds fish at midday.

Fishermen catch crappies around a variety of man-made objects. Bridges, piers, docks and submerged features like roadbeds, building foundations and fencelines will hold fish at some time of the year.

Fish attractors, especially brush piles, produce crappies more consistently than other man-made features. Fisheries agencies often place brush piles in reservoirs where trees and other cover were removed before the lake was formed. Many fishermen make their own brush piles, then sink them off the end of a dock or along a drop-off. Other attractors include hay bales, tires, stakebeds and crib shelters.

Because of the crappie's roving nature, attractors that hold fish one day may be worthless the next. In lakes with many submerged brush piles, fishermen often establish *milk runs,* moving from one pile to the next until they find fish.

Most anglers use a bobber and minnow when fishing a brush pile. The fish generally hold in a small area, so still-fishing produces more fish than casting or trolling. But the angler who can work a small jig over the brushtops without snagging will usually catch more crappies than the still-fisherman.

BRUSH PILES are excellent crappie producers, especially if they stand several feet above bottom and have many openings between the branches. Look for brush piles on bald humps or along drop-offs with little cover. Fish attractors placed in areas with abundant cover seldom draw large numbers of crappies.

RIPRAP often holds crappies in spring. The rocks absorb sunlight and warm the surrounding water, attracting baitfish and other crappie foods.

BOAT HARBORS, channels and canals also warm quickly in spring. Look for crappies along sunny shorelines protected from the wind.

BOATHOUSES, docks and swimming platforms attract crappies. During summer, the most productive structures are in water at least 10 feet deep.

BRIDGE PILINGS provide shade for crappies, especially if they have numerous cross-members. Algae growth on wooden pilings draws insects that attract baitfish.

FISHING LOUNGES offer good crappie action because operators often drop chum into the area. Most lounges have covered tops and are heated during cold weather.

How to Fish Bridges

CAST beyond a piling, then retrieve the lure or bait as close to the piling as possible. Or bump the piling to create an erratic action that may trigger a strike.

DROP a ⅛- or ¼-ounce jigging spoon into the shade next to a piling. Jig vertically at different depths to find fish. Work the lure alongside any cross-members.

How to Fish a Floating Dock

CAST a small jig off one side of a floating dock. Strip off line as the lure sinks to bottom.

HOLD your rod tip under the surface, then swing it around the end of the dock. Walk to the opposite side.

RETRIEVE the jig so it passes below the dock. This may be the only way to reach fish hiding underneath.

How to Fish Docks With Posts

BOUNCE a small jig off bottom while walking slowly along the dock. Keep the lure close to the edge and work each post thoroughly.

LOWER a bobber and minnow off the upwind side of a dock. Allow the wind to push the float under the dock to reach crappies in the shade.

How to Fish a Brush Pile

ANCHOR your boat within casting distance on the downwind side of a brush pile. If your anchor pulls loose, the boat will not drift over the brush and spook the fish.

CAST a minnow and small float beyond the brush pile. Let the wind drift the bait over and alongside the brush. Land fish quickly so they will not tangle in the branches.

How to Make a Brush Pile

BUNDLE fresh branches with plastic bailing twine or copper wire. Tie on a cement block. Do not pack the branches too tightly; crappies prefer large openings.

SINK a discarded Christmas tree by wedging the trunk into the hole of a heavy cement block. Lash the tree in place, then drop it into the water.

How to Make Other Fish Attractors

BUILD a stakebed with a 4×8-foot frame made of 2×4s. Use 1×2 uprights that are 4 to 7 feet long. Place two, 40-pound blocks over the stakes in each corner.

TIE three tires together with nylon rope. Drill holes in the tops of the tires so air can escape. Wedge a cement block into each tire.

Fishing for Suspended Crappies

Crappies have a greater tendency to suspend than any other panfish. Fishermen commonly find the fish hanging in mid-water, sometimes far from structure or cover. They will suspend in any season but mainly during summer.

Schools of crappies suspend to feed on plankton or on small baitfish that gather to eat the minute organisms. Most types of plankton are sensitive to light. They move shallower in the evening and deeper at midday.

When crappies are hanging over open water, you may waste a lot of time searching for them. A depth finder will improve your odds dramatically. Many fishermen troll or drift along a breakline, periodically changing depths until they find the fish.

How Crappies Suspend

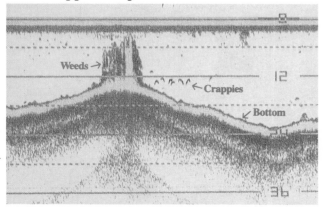

HORIZONTAL layering usually takes place just off a weedline at the same depth as the base of the weeds. Crappies may move away from the weeds and form a horizontal layer in open water.

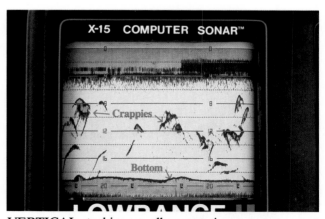

VERTICAL stacking usually occurs in open water, not far from some type of structure. This graph tape shows crappies suspended from just above bottom to within 7 feet of the surface.

The Yo-Yo Technique

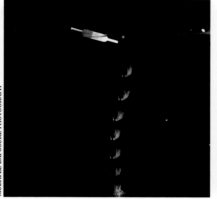

MULTIPLE EXPOSURE PHOTOGRAPH

TIE on a jig with a marabou or soft plastic tail below a slip-bobber. Adjust the bobber stop so the jig hangs at the depth of the fish.

CAST into the vicinity of the suspended crappies. Strip line from your reel so the jig can slide freely through the slip-bobber.

RETRIEVE slowly with jerks and pauses. With each jerk, the line slides up through the float. Crappies strike when the jig sinks.

How to Troll for Suspended Crappies

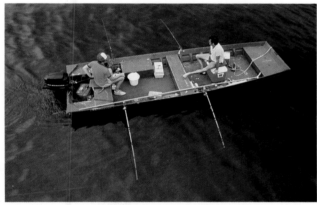

PLACE several long poles in rod holders so the tips ride 1 to 2 feet above the water. Many fishermen use 12-foot extension poles with jig-minnow combinations or tandem hook rigs baited with minnows.

TROLL slowly along a drop-off with each bait running at a different depth. If one of the rods produces more crappies than the others, set the other rods to fish the same depth.

The Countdown Method for Suspended Crappies

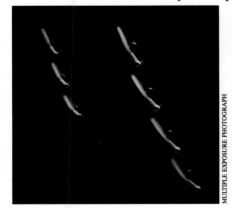

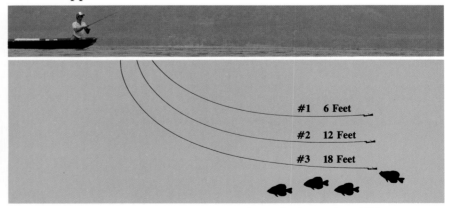

MULTIPLE EXPOSURE PHOTOGRAPH

CAST a jig, then count as it sinks. With 6-pound line, a 1/32-ounce marabou jig (left) drops about 1 foot in one second; a 1/8-ounce jig (right) about 2 feet.

BEGIN your retrieve at different counts until you find crappies. With a 1/8-ounce jig, retrieve #1 (started at 3 seconds) and retrieve #2 (6 seconds) pass too far above the fish. But retrieve #3 (9 seconds) draws a strike. If you know where fish are located, count down to 1 to 2 feet above that depth.

Night Fishing for Crappies

On warm summer evenings, fishermen crowd the docks of many southern reservoirs. Night fishing is popular because anglers can escape the sweltering daytime heat and enjoy fast crappie action. In a study on a California reservoir, summertime anglers caught crappies 16 times faster at night than they did during the day.

Fishermen use lights to attract minnows, which in turn draw crappies. Most bring their own lanterns or floating lights, but some fish at docks with permanently-mounted floodlights.

Night fishing is best during the dark of the moon. Lights draw fewer fish on moonlit nights. Crappies generally begin to bite just after dark. Good fishing usually lasts one to two hours, although the fish may continue to bite through the night. Night-fishing success tapers off in fall.

Most night fishing takes place around docks, piers, bridges and other easy-to-reach places. But some veteran anglers prefer tree lines or creek channel edges that can be reached only by boat. Almost all night fishermen use live minnows on bobber rigs.

Lights for Night Fishing

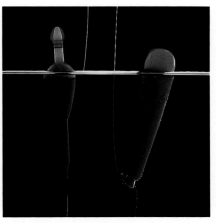

GAS LANTERNS and battery-powered fluorescent lamps provide enough light to draw minnows. But they also attract swarms of insects.

FLOATING LIGHTS draw minnows, but not pesky insects. This model is supported by a styrofoam ring and powered by a car battery.

LIGHTED BOBBERS help detect bites if you do not have a lantern. Tiny lithium batteries provide power. Some can be rigged as slip-floats.

How to Rig and Use a Lantern

SUSPEND a lantern on a board or pole so it hangs just above the water. Some anglers use commercial lantern hangers which clamp onto the side of the boat. Fish around the edge of the lighted area, because crappies will not feed in intense light. Experiment with different depths to find the fish.

TIE your lantern to a limb along a steep bank. Anchor away from the light and use a long fishing pole. This prevents you from spooking the fish and enables you to stay away from insects that swarm around the light.

DIRECT the light downward by making a lantern shield from a circle of tinfoil. Cut out the center and a wedge from one side. Wrap the foil around the lantern just under the vents, then crimp the edge at the seam.

White Bass

All About White Bass

Few gamefish provide as much angling excitement as white bass. The silvery fish cruise about in schools that may cover several acres. Fishermen who find these huge schools often enjoy spectacular fishing.

Originally found in the Great Lakes, St. Lawrence River and the Mississippi River system, white bass have been successfully stocked in many other regions, particularly the Southeast and Southwest. Commonly introduced in new reservoirs, they provide excellent fishing two to three years after stocking.

White bass thrive in lakes and reservoirs connected to large river systems. They prefer relatively clear waters with gravel, sand or rock bottoms. But they also live in murky waters. Unlike sunfish and crappies, white bass rarely seek cover. Instead, they spend most of their time in open water from 10 to 30 feet deep.

A member of the *temperate bass* family, the white bass has several close relatives including the white perch (page 127), yellow bass and the striped bass. In the 1960s, fisheries biologists first crossed male white bass with female striped bass to produce an aggressive, extremely fast-growing hybrid. These fish are being stocked in many warmwater reservoirs throughout the South.

Often called *sand bass, striper* or *silver bass,* the white bass has silvery sides laced with rows of dark lines. Its belly is white, but the back may vary from bluish-gray to dark green.

White bass rely primarily on eyesight for chasing and catching their prey. In most waters, they feed almost exclusively on small shad, when they are available. They also eat emerald shiners and other small fish, in addition to crayfish, mollusks, worms and insects. White bass gorge themselves on mayflies during a hatch.

In waters with large populations of shad, white bass grow quickly. In warm, southern reservoirs, a fish may reach 1 pound after just two years. But white bass do not attain large sizes, because they seldom live longer than six years.

Most white bass caught by angling weigh between 1 and 2 pounds. The world record, taken from the Colorado River, Texas in 1977, weighed 5 pounds, 9 ounces.

White bass spawn in tributary streams of large lakes and reservoirs, typically in water 58° to 64°F. They do not build nests. The female deposits her eggs in the current, while the male releases his sperm, fertilizing the eggs as they sink. The eggs stick to gravel, rocks or vegetation where they normally hatch within 24 to 48 hours. A female may deposit more than a half-million eggs.

Spawning activity usually lasts five to ten days. Parents do not guard the eggs, but begin migrating back to the lake.

After hatching, the tiny fry form dense schools, a characteristic that white bass exhibit all of their lives. The schools move about constantly, some roaming as much as seven miles a day. Tagged white bass have been found over 100 miles away from where they were marked.

White Bass Range

WHITE BASS have five to seven unbroken horizontal stripes above the lateral line. Stripes below the lateral line are usually faint and may be broken. The two dorsal fins are not joined at the base.

CLOSE RELATIVES of the white bass include (1) white perch, which lack the horizontal stripes of other temperate bass; (2) yellow bass, which resemble white bass in body shape but have dorsal fins joined slightly at the base; (3) striped bass, which have a slimmer body and distinct, unbroken stripes below the lateral line.

Where to Find White Bass

Each spring, as the water temperature approaches 50°F, white bass move from deep wintering areas in lakes and reservoirs toward the rivers and creeks where their lives began. They stage at the mouths of these tributaries, usually in 10- to 25-foot deep holes adjacent to shallow flats with sand or gravel bottoms. In reservoirs, these staging areas are usually in the upper portion of the lake.

As the water temperature climbs above 50°F, white bass begin migrating upriver to spawn. The males usually precede the females by several days or even a week. Fishermen begin lining the riverbanks early, but the best fishing does not start until the water exceeds 55°F.

The fish continue moving upstream until blocked by a dam, waterfall or shallow water. Huge concentrations of white bass form in tailraces below large dams. Many fish spawn in the tailraces, often over submerged rock islands and sandbars, or in riprap along shore. Most white bass deposit their eggs in 5 to 10 feet of water.

White bass move back toward the main lake during severe cold fronts or when heavy rains muddy the water. But they usually return once the weather warms and the stream begins to clear.

After spawning, both male and female white bass migrate back to their pre-spawn staging areas. There, they may linger several days or even weeks before filtering into the main body of the reservoir.

Locating white bass can be difficult during summer. You may find them at almost any depth, and they seldom remain in one spot very long. Unlike most fish, they do not hold tight to structure. However, creek channels, roads and ridges may serve as

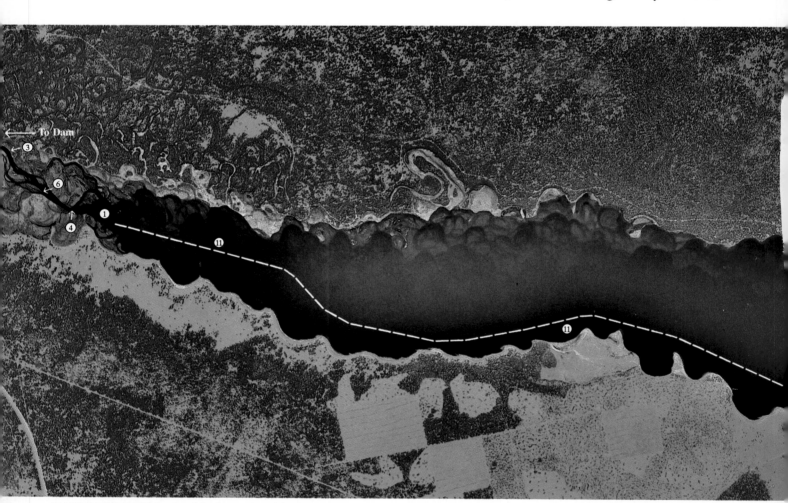

EARLY SPRING finds white bass near (1) the mouth of the main river feeding the reservoir and (2) mouths of creek arms with inflowing water. As they move upstream, they concentrate near (3) outside bends of the main river and (4) points in both the main river and creek arms. Most spawn in the tailrace below the dam (not shown). Some fish spawn in (5) streams flowing into back ends of the arms or (6) in eddies below islands and sandbars.

92

underwater highways for the schools. Reservoir fishermen may troll for miles to locate a school along a breakline.

Many lakes and reservoirs form thermoclines in summer. In these waters, white bass often suspend along the upper edge of the thermocline, where the water is cool but still contains oxygen.

Through summer and fall, white bass attack schools of shad on the surface, especially in morning or early evening. Most anglers look for large gravel or sand flats adjacent to deep water. Some of the best flats top off at 6 to 10 feet. Many anglers catch white bass on sand or mud deltas along the mouths of tributary streams. The best deltas drop off sharply, so the fish can reach deep water quickly. White bass will push baitfish toward lines of trees or brush, or onto shallow beaches. Many public beaches offer excellent fishing just after they close for the season.

White bass often feed at night during summer and early fall. Anglers work schools on gravel flats or

sunken islands, usually in 10 to 20 feet of water, but occasionally as shallow as 3 feet. Shore fishermen catch white bass at night along riprap banks or near piers and bridges.

After the fall turnover, white bass spend more time in deeper water, but continue to chase baitfish on or near the surface. They feed in the same general areas where they were found during summer.

In winter, white bass collect in deep water off sunken islands, humps and ridges, often at the lower end of the reservoir. They do not travel as widely as they did in summer, but will move vertically to feed, especially after several warm days. Once the water temperature slips below 50°F, white bass eat very little. Many anglers continue to find good fishing in warmwater discharges below power plants. The fish feed all winter in these areas.

Throughout the year, white bass are most active during stable weather or on overcast, breezy days when clouds and waves reduce light penetration.

NASA HIGH ALTITUDE PHOTOGRAPH

SUMMER-FALL locations are usually in or near the main body of the lake. They include: (7) sand or gravel flats near deep water, (8) submerged point, (9) large, shallow point, (10) edges of creek channel (small dashes), (11) edges of main river channel (large dashes), (12) riprap banks. LATE FALL-WINTER locations include: (13) deep areas next to islands, (14) deep water just off flats, (15) main river channel, (16) deep areas of creek channel.

Fishing for White Bass

White bass feed in packs, pushing baitfish to the surface or into confined areas, then slashing into their prey. Anglers who work these rampaging schools often catch fish on every cast.

But fishing for white bass is not always easy. They can be extremely selective about the size of lure they strike. And whites spook more easily than other panfish. When you find a school, you must keep your distance or the fish will quickly disappear.

White bass put up a strong fight when hooked on light tackle. Six- to eight-pound line works well in most situations, but you should check the line frequently for cuts. Their razor sharp gill covers may nick the line, causing it to snap at the slightest tug.

Weather has little effect on white bass fishing, although surface-feeding may last longer on overcast days. White bass usually continue to feed despite cold front conditions.

MULTIPLE EXPOSURE PHOTOGRAPH

FAST RETRIEVES generally work best for white bass, because the fish are accustomed to chasing fast-moving

WHITE BASS school according to size. If you locate a school and begin catching small fish, chances are you will continue to catch only small fish. Instead, try to find another school.

WATCH for swirls, slurps or splashes, signs that white bass are feeding on the surface. Fishermen routinely look for circling gulls to find schools of bass surface-feeding on shad (page 100).

94

prey in open water. Quite often, an angler will draw his lure slowly through a school, then begin reeling quickly as he nears the end of his retrieve. White bass strike just before he pulls the lure from the water.

APPROACH white bass quietly. They will move away from the sound of an outboard or the clanking of gear on the bottom of the boat. Use an electric trolling motor or drift along the edge of the school.

AVOID grabbing a white bass across the gill plates. Each plate has a needle-sharp spine (arrow) that can inflict a painful wound. Instead, hold the fish by the lower lip or grip it firmly across the back.

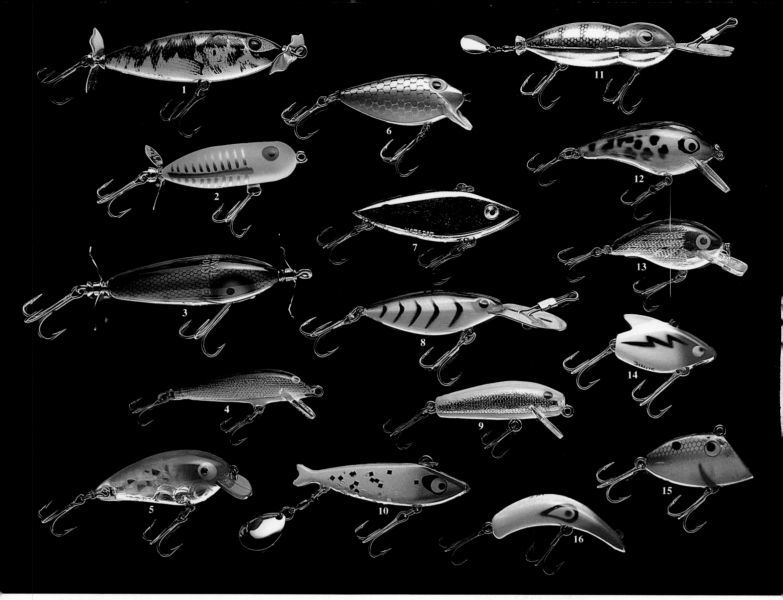

LURES for white bass include: (1) Crazy Shad®, (2) Tiny Torpedo®, (3) Spin-I-Diddee®, (4) Floating Rapala®, (5) Big Jim™, (6) Thin Fin® XT™, (7) Th' Spot®, (8) Hot 'N Tot®, (9) A.C. Shiner, (10) Tail Gater, (11) Hellbender, (12) Bo-Jack, (13) Teeny-R®, (14) Sonic®, (15) Bayou Boogie, (16) Lazy Ike, (17) Aglia®, (18) Shyster®, (19)

Lures for White Bass

White bass will strike almost any kind of lure, provided it is similar in size to their food.

Shad, an important food item, usually hatch in late spring or early summer and grow rapidly through fall. But some shad continue to hatch throughout summer. This complicates lure selection, because the size of shad eaten by white bass may change from day to day. Injured shad on the surface or regurgitated shad in a live well may provide a clue to lure size.

Asked to choose an all-around white bass lure, most veteran fishermen would name the jig. You can bump a jig along bottom for deep-running whites, or crank it across the surface when the fish are breaking water. And you can remove a jig hook from a fish's mouth in seconds and get your line back into the water.

In many southern reservoirs, tailspins rival jigs in popularity. Like jigs, tailspins can be fished shallow or deep, but the spinner blade provides flash that jigs lack.

The tailspin is an excellent choice for vertical jigging, because the spinner helicopters as the lure

Cottontail®, (20) Little Suzy™, (21) Little George, (22) Sonar™, (23) Slab Spoon®, (24) Gay Blade®, (25) Krocodile®, (26) Hopkins Shorty®, (27) Mepps® Spoon, (28) Little Cleo®, (29) Dardevle Imp Klicker®, (30) Twister® Meeny, (31) Fuzz-E-Grub®, (32) Whistler®, (33) Road Runner®, (34) Maribou Jig.

drops. This slows the lure's descent, giving the fish more time to strike. Anglers also use vibrating blades and jigging spoons for vertical jigging.

Crankbaits work well when white bass are scattered because they enable you to cover a lot of water. Any crankbait will work, but many fishermen prefer models with tight, vibrating actions and rattle chambers. The vibration and noise may coax white bass to strike.

Some anglers cast small, thick-bodied spoons. These artificial lures can be tossed long distances, enabling fishermen to avoid spooking surface-feeding bass.

White bass will also strike fly lures, especially streamers that resemble minnows. Fishermen sometimes jerk poppers violently across the surface to incite a feeding frenzy.

During a mayfly hatch, white bass feed heavily on emerging nymphs. Anglers often have trouble catching fish when a hatch is in progress. But bass will strike a fly that imitates the emerging insect. When fly-fishing, a sinking line usually works better than a floating one.

Some anglers attach a popping plug just ahead of the lure. The plug adds weight for casting and keeps the lure near the surface. The popping sounds help to attract fish.

A few anglers prefer minnows for white bass. But live bait takes longer to rig, costing you valuable time when fish are biting.

DAMS halt the progress of white bass moving upstream to spawn. The fish deposit their eggs at night, usually in the main current. During the day, they hang in eddies just to the side of fast-moving water.

Fishing for Spawning White Bass

Spawning time offers the easiest white bass fishing of the year. Tailraces come alive with fish and the angler has only to look or listen for swirling bass, then toss a lure somewhere near. It is not uncommon for a fisherman to catch 50 to 100 whites a day at the peak of the spawning run.

But fishing for spawning whites can be frustrating. Even when bass are churning the water, they may ignore your lure. You can often entice these fish to strike by switching to a very small lure, like a 1/16-ounce jig.

Fishermen begin catching white bass several weeks before spawning time. The fish start moving up-stream when the water reaches the low 50s. As white bass migrate, they gather in eddies, isolated bays, and other slow-current areas just off the main channel. They usually hold at depths of 5 to 15 feet during the pre-spawn period, but may move into holes as deep as 25 feet during cold snaps.

White bass gather in their spawning areas when water temperatures reach the upper 50s. Look for fish in eddies closer to the dam, often in water only 1 to 3 feet deep.

Most fish spawn at night or during evening hours. When ready to spawn, a female swims toward the surface, attracting several males. During the spawning act, the fish thrash and roll on the water. Night-time anglers listen for the spawning fish, then cast toward the sound.

Not all white bass swim upstream to spawn. In reservoirs, some fish spawn on sand or gravel shoals near the upper end of the main lake. These areas hold many spawners in low-water years when the streams do not have enough current to attract fish. In Lake Erie, most fish spawn in the major tributaries, but some deposit their eggs on large, off-shore reefs that top off at 5 to 10 feet.

Where to Find White Bass During the Spawning Period

FLOODED WILLOWS attract white bass moving upstream. The fish hold at the base of the willows in water 5 feet or less.

LOG JAMS, fallen trees and other obstructions break the current. White bass congregate in slack-water holding areas just downstream.

SMALL CREEKS flowing into the upper end of a reservoir or a spawning stream will draw bass, especially if they have clear water.

How to Fish an Eddy

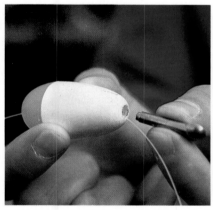

ATTACH a casting bobber 2 feet ahead of a small jig. The bobber adds casting weight and attracts bass as you jerk it across the surface.

CAST the bobber rig into the area where white bass are working. Some anglers use a two-handed cast to reach fish far from shore.

ALLOW the current to sweep your rig in a large circle around the eddy. Twitch the rod frequently to give the jig more action.

How to Drift for Spawning White Bass

DRIFT with the current while one person bumps a jig along bottom and the other casts toward shore. Keep moving until you find the fish.

HOLD the boat in position when you locate white bass. Point the bow upstream and adjust your throttle to counteract the current.

Jump-fishing for White Bass

For fast action, nothing rivals jump-fishing for white bass. Huge schools of bass herd baitfish, especially shad, to the surface. Attracted by the commotion, gulls swoop down to grab baitfish injured by the feeding bass.

Jump-fishing refers to the technique for catching white bass when they attack, or *jump*, baitfish on the surface. Anglers look for circling gulls or signs of feeding white bass. Once they spot a school, they quickly motor toward it. Most fishermen cast shallow-running lures into the fish. When the school sounds, they begin vertical jigging with heavy spoons or jigs.

Fishing the jumps generally peaks in fall, when shad form dense schools that feed on plankton near the surface. But in some waters, jump-fishing begins in early summer, when white bass feed on hatching mayflies or small minnows. Anglers often find surface-feeding whites on sand or gravel flats less than 10 feet deep.

In clear weather, jump-fishing is best early and late in the day. Whites may feed all day under cloudy skies. Windy conditions make it difficult to spot fish that are feeding on the surface.

White bass spook easily when surface-feeding. Move in quietly and do not anchor. A heavy lure enables you to cast farther, so you can stay away from the school.

WATCH for gulls swooping down to catch injured shad,

How to Fish the Jumps

Wind Direction →

MOTOR quickly to the feeding area when you spot a flock of circling and diving gulls. A school may feed for only a few minutes. If you hesitate, the fish may be gone when you arrive.

STOP short of the school to avoid spooking the fish. Cut the motor on the upwind side and let the boat glide into position. Be ready to cast as soon as you reach the school; the first few casts are the most productive.

or look for white bass breaking the surface. Many jump-fishermen use binoculars to spot the action from a distance.

DRIFT along the edge of the feeding area while casting into the school. Use an electric trolling motor or oars to control the path of the drift. Try to keep the boat just within casting distance.

START the engine when the boat drifts too far from the school. Swing away from the feeding area, then head upwind and drift back again. Never run the motor through a school of feeding bass.

How to Get the Most Fish Out of a School

When a school of white bass breaks water, be ready to take advantage of the situation because the fish can disappear quickly. The following techniques will improve your jump-fishing success.

How to Rig and Use a Double Jig

TIE a three-way swivel to your line. Attach 6- and 10-inch droppers of 12-pound mono to the swivel, then tie a ¼-ounce jig on each dropper.

RETRIEVE the jig through a school. When a fish grabs one jig, the commotion attracts other fish which strike the trailing jig.

SWING the fish into the boat with a smooth motion. If you net them, you may tangle the lines and lose valuable fishing time.

How to Fish a School After it Sounds

LOOK for gulls resting on the surface, then work the area thoroughly. The birds will usually remain after the school sounds.

TROLL along the edge of a flat where white bass were surfacing. The fish often remain in the vicinity, but drop into deeper water after they feed. Bounce a lead-head jig or tailspin slowly along the drop-off while watching for fish on your depth finder.

Tips for Jump-fishing

FLATTEN your barbs with a pliers. This enables you to unhook white bass quickly and catch more before the school disappears.

REPLACE trebles with single hooks or clip off two of the hooks with a wire cutter. These techniques also let you unhook white bass faster.

HOOK a white bass, then let it fight while you keep a tight line. Because of their competitive nature, other bass swarm toward the hooked fish. Sometimes several fish follow within inches in an attempt to steal the lure.

WAIT a few seconds before reeling to give your partner time to cast toward your hooked bass. When he hooks a fish, quickly land your fish and cast toward his. Continue this tactic as long as white bass remain in the area.

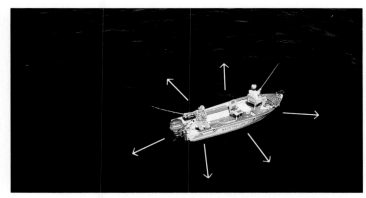

FAN-CAST with a crankbait while drifting over the area where bass were feeding. If nothing bites, try a drift off to each side. If fish are still in the area, a fast-moving lure will usually trigger a strike.

DRAW white bass back to the surface with a noisy topwater lure. A small jig trailing 1 to 2 feet behind the lure will catch fish attracted by the commotion. Sometimes the entire school will resume surface-feeding.

CARRY several rods rigged with your favorite lures for jump-fishing. If you snap your line or switch to a different presentation, you will not have to waste time retying.

TOSS white bass into a cooler partially filled with ice. They die quickly on a stringer. A cooler keeps them fresh and saves time that would be wasted stringing fish.

Night Fishing for White Bass

During the heat of summer, you can often improve your white bass success by fishing after dark. Night fishing also works well at spawning time, but most anglers catch all the fish they want during the day.

Night fishing for white bass and crappies has many similarities. It is not unusual for fishermen to catch a mixed bag. During summer, anglers use lights to concentrate fish. Dark nights are best; the lights may not attract fish during a full moon. Minnows work well for both species, but white bass will also strike jigs.

The bridges, piers and lighted docks that produce crappies at night may also yield white bass. Other good locations include the edges of creek and river channels, drop-offs adjacent to sand flats and the mouths of creek arms.

White bass may feed at any time during the night. Most fishermen anchor in a spot that has produced in the past and wait for the fish to move in. The bass generally arrive at the same location at the same hour several nights in succession. If the fish do not show up, try locating them with a graph recorder or a flasher.

Some night fishermen use a handline baited with a minnow. A handline enables you to detect bites easily, even in darkness.

How to Make a Lighted Slip-bobber

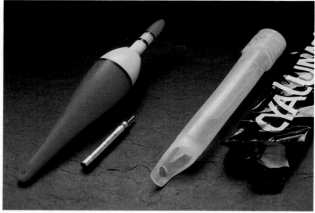

BUY a lighted slip-bobber (left) powered by a lithium battery or make your own float with a 4-inch Cyalume® light stick (right). The stick will protrude just above the surface and will glow from 8 to 12 hours.

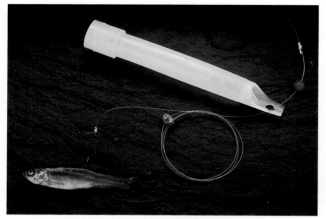

TIE a lighted slip-bobber rig by first attaching a bobber stop. Thread on a small bead so the knot cannot slip through the hole in the bobber. Add a #4 hook and enough split-shot to balance the bobber.

How to Make and Use a Handline

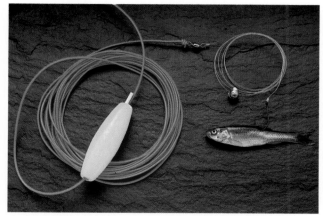

THREAD a small peg bobber on No. 5 or No. 6 sinking fly line. Tie the line to one end of a barrel swivel and 4 feet of 6-pound mono to the other end. Pinch on a split-shot, then add a #4 hook and a minnow.

DRAPE the line over the side so the bobber hangs along the inside of the boat. Watch the bobber closely for any movement. The fly line will slide easily up the side when a white bass strikes.

LIGHTS play an important role in night fishing for white bass. Baitfish drawn to the light will eventually attract bass. Most fishermen use gas lanterns. Others prefer floating crappie lights (page 86) or submerged lights be-cause they draw fewer insects and add more illumination to the water. In murky water, white bass will move into the beam of light. In clear water, they generally remain around the dimly-lit perimeter.

Tips for Night Fishing

SET the depth with a bobberless rig by counting the number of times you turn the reel handle to reach the proper depth. Then you can return your lure or bait to the same depth after you catch a fish.

SINK a headlight in a wire cage to attract bass. Grease the headlight contacts to prevent electrolytic corrosion, then run wires to a car battery. Add enough lead weight to sink the light, then lower it about 4 to 6 feet.

Fishing for White Bass in Warmwater Discharges

Warmwater discharges from power plants offer excellent, but often overlooked fishing opportunities. The plants draw water from rivers or lakes to cool their turbines, then return the heated water. White bass begin congregating around discharge areas in late fall, when the water temperature of rivers and lakes drops below 50°F. The fish remain until spring.

Heated discharges also attract shad and other bass foods. White bass feed actively through the winter, because the warm water keeps their metabolism at a high level.

Because the fish are active, anglers should use a moderately fast retrieve. The fish usually ignore slow-moving lures. The best lures include small crankbaits, spoons and jigs.

Most power plants allow fishing in the discharge areas. Some even provide parking areas, launching ramps and other facilities for the angler's convenience. To find out about warmwater discharges in your area, call the public relations office of your local power company.

DISCHARGE CANALS carry water as much as 40 degrees warmer than the river or lake. Most anglers fish from shore, but some use small boats.

EDDIES near the upstream end of the canal usually harbor the most white bass. Fishermen also catch bass in slow-moving water farther downstream.

Fishing for White Bass in Deep Water

White bass move to the depths in summer to escape warm surface waters. It is not unusual to find schools of bass in water as deep as 30 feet. But in late fall and winter, the depths become slightly warmer than water at the surface. White bass are drawn to the warmer water, sometimes to depths of 50 feet or more.

When white bass move to deep water, most fishermen give up and concentrate on other types of fish. But you can still catch white bass, and often in good numbers, if you use the proper techniques.

In summer, white bass seldom stay in one spot for long. They follow schools of shad, so you must cover a lot of water to find the fish. Most anglers troll with deep-running lures, always watching their depth finders for schools.

In late fall and winter, white bass form tighter schools and stay in one area for long periods. They feed very little and seldom chase fast-moving lures. Anglers mark the schools carefully, then catch the fish by vertical jigging.

DEEP-DIVING LURES, when trolled at high speed, catch white bass in summer. Some fishermen attach trailing jigs or spinners to tempt more strikes.

VERTICAL JIGGING may be the only way to catch white bass in late fall and winter. Jig at or slightly above the level of the fish, as shown on this graph tape.

METERED LEAD-CORE LINE enables you to troll in deep water. When you hook a fish, note the color of the line so you can return to the same depth.

All About Yellow Perch

Fillets of yellow perch command a high price at the market. If you have ever tasted them, you know why. But once you have seen a swarm of tiny yellow perch following your bait, you can also understand why some fishermen consider them to be bait-stealing pests.

The yellow perch is a mid-sized member of the perch family. Most fish caught by anglers are 6 to 9 inches long. Any perch larger than 9 inches or ½ pound is considered a *jumbo*. Of the 100 other species in the perch family, most are darters that seldom grow longer than 3 inches. At the other extreme is the walleye, which can exceed 15 pounds.

Perch were originally found in the north central and northeastern states and in all of the Canadian provinces with the exception of British Columbia. Widespread stocking has expanded their range as far south as New Mexico and Texas. Yellow perch continue to spread naturally into many new waters.

Good-sized yellow perch abound in relatively clear, cool lakes and reservoirs with sand, gravel or rock bottoms and moderate vegetation. Weedy, mud-bottomed lakes sometimes have large populations, but smaller fish. The dense weeds provide cover where young perch can escape predators. Too many perch survive, resulting in stunted fish that rarely grow larger than a few ounces.

Yellow perch thrive in the Great Lakes, with the exception of Lake Superior. They are also found in the brackish waters of Atlantic Coast estuaries, in large rivers, and occasionally in deep ponds.

Unlike crappies, perch are comfortable in bright light. In fact, they cannot see well in dim light, which explains why they are easy prey for night-feeding predators such as the walleye. Anglers rarely catch yellow perch after dark.

Most yellow perch spawn at night or early in the morning, normally in water 43° to 48°F. Several males will flank a female, then release their milt as she deposits her eggs. The eggs are clustered within jelly-like bands, called *egg strands*, that cling to weeds, brush and debris.

The eggs hatch in 10 to 14 days. The newly-hatched fry move to open water where they remain for several weeks. Then, they return to the shallows, forming huge schools that provide a lush food supply for predator fish. As the perch grow, they begin spending more time in deeper areas of the lake.

The diet of perch changes as they grow larger. Young fish feed on zooplankton and the larvae of aquatic insects. Adult perch eat small minnows and crustaceans, snails, leeches and other invertebrates.

Yellow perch in northern waters grow more slowly but live longer than perch in the southern parts of their range. Few yellow perch live longer than 9 or 10 years. The world record, 4 pounds, 3 ounces, was caught in 1865 from the Delaware River in New Jersey.

Yellow Perch Range

YELLOW PERCH, sometimes called *raccoon* or *ringed perch*, are strikingly marked with six to nine greenish-black or olive vertical bars on each side. The back may be black or dark olive-green, while the belly varies from pale yellow to white. The perch has two separate dorsal fins and its tail fin is distinctly forked.

EGG STRANDS of perch are translucent, varying from white to yellow. A typical strand is about 1 inch wide, 6 to 12 inches long and contains about 20,000 eggs.

SCHOOLS of perch are made up of fish similar in age and size. Schools of jumbo perch usually hug bottom in open water.

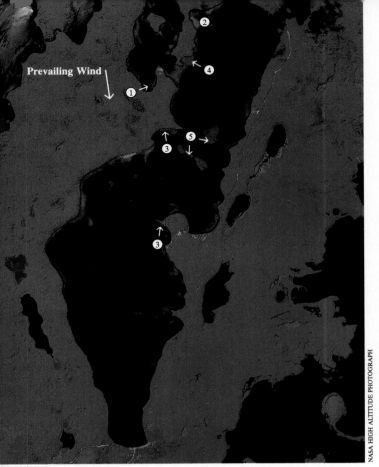

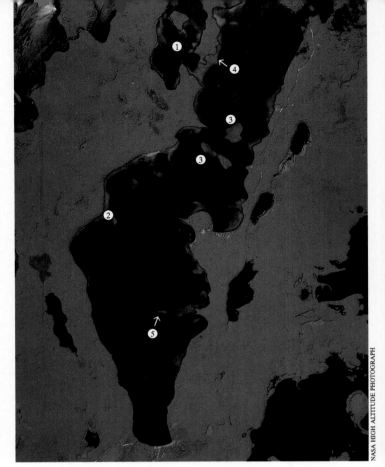

SPAWNING AREAS for yellow perch in natural lakes include: (1) isolated bays with scattered weeds, (2) main lake bays, (3) shallow water on protected side of points, (4) shoreline shoals, (5) tops of mid-lake reefs.

LATE SPRING-SUMMER locations include: (1) deeper portions of spawning bays, (2) shoreline points, (3) drop-offs along mid-lake reefs, (4) edges of shoreline shoals with submerged weeds, (5) submerged points.

Where to Find Yellow Perch

Finding small yellow perch can be as easy as dangling a worm off most any dock. But the angler looking for jumbo perch faces more of a challenge.

SPRING. Yellow perch begin moving out of deep wintering areas toward shallower water in early spring. In the southern part of their range and along the Atlantic Coast, spawning migrations begin as early as late February. Perch in northern lakes start their spawning runs in mid-April or early May.

Perch often migrate long distances, sometimes 20 miles or more, to reach their spawning grounds. In the Great Lakes, most perch spend their entire lives

in large, warmwater bays. These fish edge out of deep water near rock reefs and islands onto reef edges. Others move into the mouths of tributaries or into man-made drainage ditches.

Perch are very selective as to where they spawn. They prefer sand, gravel or rock bottoms with scattered weeds or brush. In most lakes and reservoirs, they spawn in shallow, protected bays in water 5 to 12 feet deep. Generally, the larger the lake, the deeper they spawn. In the western basin of Lake Erie, perch spawn on off-shore reefs in 10 to 20 feet of water, and occasionally as deep as 30 feet.

Yellow perch in Chesapeake Bay and other East Coast estuaries winter in brackish water at the mouths of large tributaries. The fish move upstream after a series of balmy spring days or a warm rain. Many perch spawn just below small dams on the upper ends of the streams. Others deposit their eggs in quiet, brush-choked areas where the stream may be only 2 to 3 feet deep.

LATE SPRING AND SUMMER. After spawning, yellow perch in most natural lakes and reservoirs linger several weeks in their spawning bays. Look

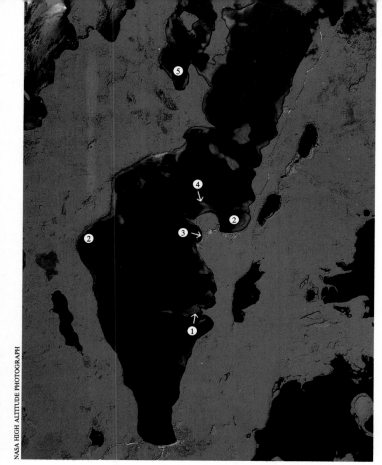

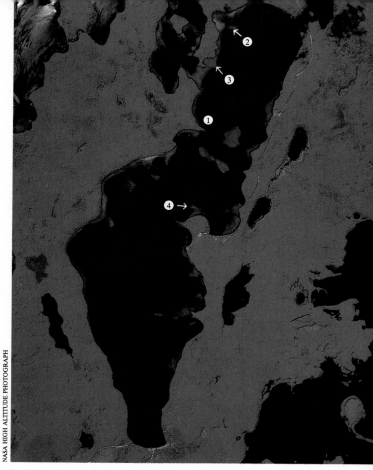

EARLY FALL locations include: (1) shallow portion of submerged point, (2) bays with sand or gravel bottoms, (3) rocky shorelines, (4) shallow flat with scattered weeds, (5) isolated bays.

LATE FALL locations for yellow perch include: (1) sharp dropping points along shore, (2) deep sunken islands, (3) deep edges of a shoreline shoal, (4) edge of a weedy flat in deep water.

for the fish in 15 to 25 feet of water. Some remain all summer unless the water becomes too warm, forcing them to find deeper, cooler water.

Jumbo perch prefer water temperatures between 65° and 70°F. Look for them in the thermocline, usually where it intersects with bottom. Some fish suspend in the thermocline over open water. Perch will also suspend in or above the thermocline to feed on plankton, baitfish or mayflies moving toward the surface to hatch.

In the Great Lakes, perch move toward open water in the bays, often gathering around rocky shoals and islands. The best reefs are isolated from other structure and have numerous projections or points. During the day, the fish feed along the points in 20 to 30 feet of water. Toward evening, they move onto the points in water as shallow as 6 feet. Great Lakes anglers also catch large yellow perch around breakwaters, pilings and docks. The best fishing spots are in 15 to 25 feet of water, with rock or sand bottoms and some vegetation.

Yellow perch in estuaries remain in the tributaries through summer. They school in deep holes at the mouths of secondary streams, or around piers, bridges and old pilings.

FALL AND WINTER. In fall, perch in deep lakes and reservoirs move into the shallows around rocky shorelines and reefs. Great Lakes fishermen record huge catches around concrete piers in only 6 to 8 feet of water. In East Coast estuaries, some fish move up secondary streams in fall. Others remain in their deep, summer locations. During winter, anglers catch few perch in waters that remain ice-free. But ice fishing (page 148) is popular on many northern lakes.

DAILY MOVEMENTS. Schools of perch begin feeding in mid-morning, once the sun has moved high enough to brighten the depths. They may continue to feed off and on throughout the day. As twilight approaches, the schools move shallower and begin to break up. Schools re-form the following morning.

Cold fronts affect yellow perch less than they do most other panfish. Even during periods of extreme cold, anglers find and catch perch in the same areas they fished during mild weather.

Fishing for Yellow Perch

Luckily for fishermen, large perch are seldom found in the same areas as the tiny bait-stealers. The bigger fish generally prefer deeper water and almost always stay within inches of bottom. If you start catching small perch, move to another spot.

When you locate a school, fishing may be slow at first. But once you begin catching fish, the commotion will often draw more perch into the area and start a feeding frenzy. If this happens, land your fish quickly and get your line back into the water, because another perch will bite immediately.

Many perch fishermen prefer multiple-hook rigs. When a fish bites, set the hook, then leave the rig in the water. The struggling perch attracts other fish, which grab the remaining baits.

The yellow perch has a small mouth compared to the size of its body, so small hooks and baits work best. Most fishermen prefer #4 or #6 short-shank hooks. Some choose long-shank hooks because they are easier to remove from the fish.

Ice-fishing baits and lures work equally well during the open-water season. Small insect larvae, ice flies and tiny jigging lures often catch perch that only nibble at larger offerings.

Lively baits work best when perch are not actively feeding. You can also entice perch to strike by adding attractors such as spinners or colored beads. When feeding actively, the fish will readily strike small pieces of minnow. If you run out of bait, use the eye from a freshly-caught perch.

Perch sometimes grab the end of the bait, then swim off rapidly. When you set the hook, you retrieve only half a worm or a chewed-up minnow. If this happens continuously, try gently pulling the bait away from the fish. When the perch feels its meal trying to escape, it will swallow the bait.

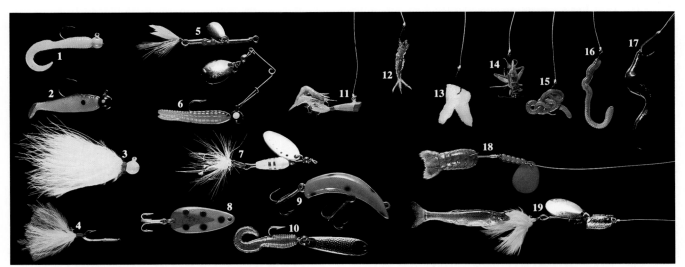

LURES AND BAITS for yellow perch include: (1) Twister® Teeny, (2) Sassy® Shad, (3) Maribou Jig, (4) no name spoon, (5) spinner/fly combo, (6) Beetle Spin™, (7) Toni™, (8) Dardevle®, (9) Lazy Ike, (10) Hopkins® ST, (11) Shad Dart with grass shrimp, (12) mayfly nymph, (13) perch meat, (14) cricket, (15) garden worm, (16) piece of nightcrawler, (17) leech, (18) snelled spinner with crayfish tail, (19) Paul Bunyan's® "66" with minnow.

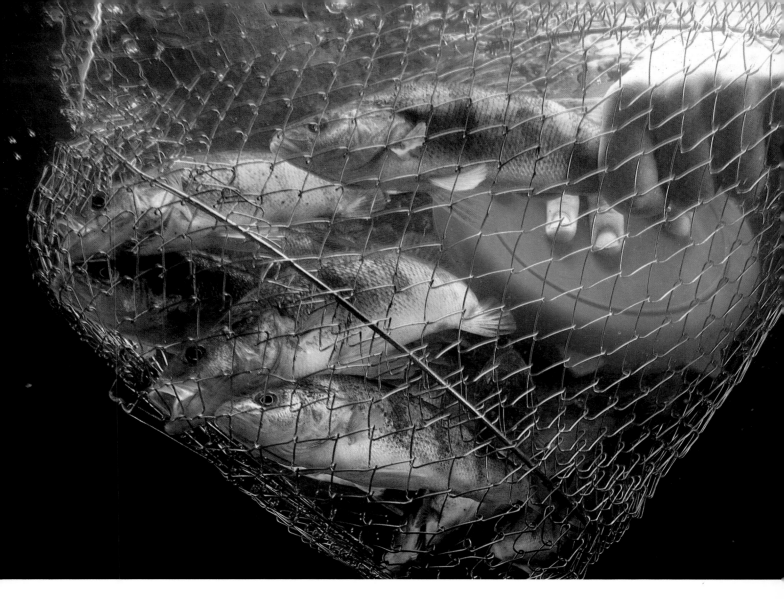

Tips for Catching Perch

MAKE a spinner rig by first threading a spinner blade and clevis onto your line. The dished side of the blade should face the hook. Add several colorful, plastic beads and a #6 hook. Bait with a worm or minnow.

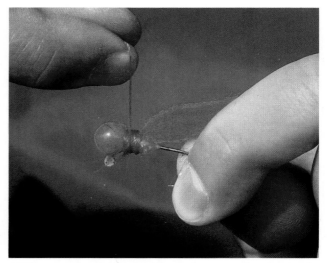

ADD several strands of bright red yarn to the shank of a plain hook or small jig. Wrap the yarn with winding thread to hold it in place. The bright color has special appeal to perch, especially during a feeding frenzy.

WEEDS and submerged branches along protected shorelines provide ideal spawning habitat, especially in natural lakes. Perch mill around these areas before spawning, then drape their eggs over the vegetation.

Fishing for Spawning Yellow Perch

When huge schools of spawning perch invade the shallows, even novice anglers fill their stringers quickly. Despite frigid water temperatures, perch bite eagerly at spawning time.

Firm, sand-gravel bottoms generally hold more spawners than soft, mucky areas. Once spawning begins, you can find the fish by looking for egg strands on shallow weeds or brush.

Most anglers use a small bobber, split-shot and a plain hook baited with a tiny minnow. Small baits and lures work best, because the fish are feeding on aquatic insects. Many fishermen prefer ice flies baited with insect larvae or bits of worm.

Fishermen on the Great Lakes use floating dropper rigs to catch perch off piers and breakwaters. These rigs can be easily adjusted so the bait is at the level of the perch. Some pier fishermen prefer spreader rigs.

In rivers and streams flowing into East Coast estuaries, anglers catch spawning perch on small, flat-headed jigs called *shad darts*. Many fishermen bait the darts with grass shrimp and suspend them from a bobber. Others combine shad darts with small spoons for extra attraction.

The techniques used to catch spawning perch also work in fall when the fish return to the shallows.

PIERS AND BREAKWALLS extending into water 20 feet or deeper attract Great Lakes perch in spring and fall. The fish move out of deep water to spawn among rocks on the inshore end of a pier.

SMALL STREAMS flowing into Atlantic Coast estuaries draw spawning perch. Look for fish in slack-water pockets or below dams. Perch move upstream on an incoming tide, downstream on an ebbing tide.

How to Make and Fish a Floating Dropper Rig

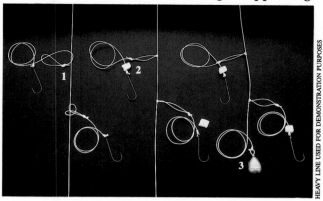

HEAVY LINE USED FOR DEMONSTRATION PURPOSES

TIE two, 6-inch monofilament leaders, each with a #6 hook on one end and a loop on the other. (1) Wrap each leader around the main line and pull the hook through the loop. (2) Thread bits of styrofoam over the hooks. (3) Add a ½-ounce bell sinker.

SPREAD the droppers 1 to 2 feet apart and bait with minnows. Cast from a pier, then tighten the line; or lower the rig over the side of the pier. The styrofoam will raise the baits slightly. If nothing bites after several minutes, slide the droppers farther up the line.

How to Make and Fish a Shad Dart Rig

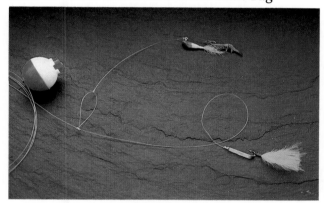

MAKE a loop (page 53) 8 inches from the end of your line. Tie a 4-inch dropper to the loop and attach a ¹⁄₁₆-ounce shad dart. Add a no name spoon, then clip on a small float. Bait the dart with a grass shrimp.

ADJUST the float so the spoon rides about 2 inches off bottom. Cast, let the rig settle, then reel back slowly with occasional twitches followed by pauses. The fluttering spoon will draw fish to the dart.

Other Popular Rigs for Perch

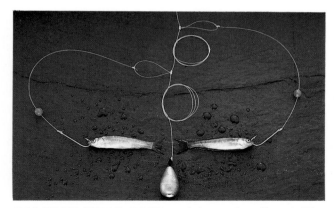

WIRE SPREADERS work well for vertical fishing because the wire keeps the baits apart. Many spreaders have spinners on the ends. Suspend a bell sinker from a piece of mono to keep the hooks above bottom.

COLORED BEAD RIGS work best when jigged. The beads will slide up the leaders, then fall back down. The extra color and action may attract yellow perch when other techniques fail.

YELLOW PERCH are drawn to bright colors. Lake Erie fishermen attach flags to their anchor ropes.

Fishing for Yellow Perch in Open Water

After spawning, large yellow perch abandon shallow cover and head for open water. They school around rock or sand-gravel reefs and sparse weedbeds. At times, they can be caught over soft, mucky bottoms, especially when mayflies or other aquatic insects are emerging from the mud.

Perch in open water normally stay near bottom at depths of 20 to 35 feet, but they may feed on reefs that top out at 10 to 15 feet. In some lakes, they suspend while feeding on plankton or schools of small baitfish.

To locate open-water perch, drift or troll slowly using a fluorescent spinner baited with a worm, minnow or strip of perch belly meat. The spinner will often catch fish that ignore other offerings. Troll just fast enough to make the blade turn.

When you find perch, a slip-bobber rig, tandem hook rig or other still-fishing technique may work better. Many fishermen prefer small jigs.

Anglers have devised some novel methods to concentrate perch. Some tie colored plastic flags to the anchor rope. Others lower pieces of metal on a rope, so they clang on the rocks. Chumming with small pieces of baitfish will attract perch and may excite them enough to trigger a feeding burst. A jigging lure spliced into the line just above the hook will also draw perch toward the bait.

118

How to Make a Trolling Rig for Perch

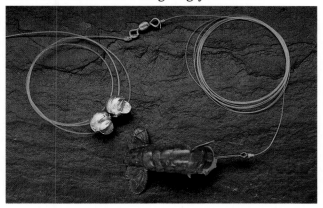

TIE on a barrel swivel, then add 2 feet of 6-pound mono. Attach a #4 or #6 hook and pinch on split-shot above the swivel. Bait with a plain or peeled crayfish tail or a minnow. The swivel prevents line twist.

How to Attract Perch With a Jigging Spoon

REMOVE the hook from a jigging lure, then tie the lure to your line. Add 12 inches of 6-pound mono to the split-ring at the bottom of the lure. Attach a #4 or #6 hook and a minnow hooked through the lips.

Other Tips for Attracting Perch

TWIST a 4- to 5-inch strip of aluminum foil around your line to attract yellow perch in open water. Some fishermen wad the foil to create rough edges that reflect light in all directions.

MAKE a line release for each rod when trolling with several lines. Open the bail, then slide a loop of line under a rubber band. When a perch strikes, it pulls the line free and can mouth the bait without feeling tension.

LOWER the jigging spoon until it touches bottom, then reel up several inches. Jig the lure up and down to attract yellow perch to the minnow. Set the hook immediately when you feel a bite.

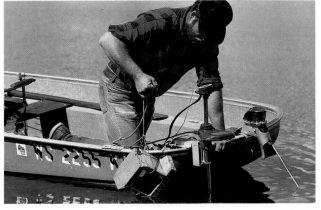

ATTACH a cement block to a rope, then lower it to bottom from an anchored boat. Tie the rope to the bow, leaving no slack. Wave action will raise and lower the block, or *mudder,* stirring up silt and attracting perch.

Other Panfish

All About Rock Bass

Many fishermen know the rock bass as the *goggle-eye* or *redeye,* names derived from the fish's bulging, reddish-colored eyes.

The rock bass is a member of the sunfish family, but is not a true bass. Its sides are mottled with dark brown on a lighter background. The fish can change color in chameleon fashion, losing its dark brown mottling in a matter of seconds.

Like most sunfish, rock bass seldom exceed 2 pounds. The world record is shared by a pair of 3-pound fish, one from the York River, Ontario in 1974 and the other from Sugar Creek, Indiana in 1979.

The original range of rock bass covered the eastern half of the United States and into southern Canada, with the exception of states along the Eastern Seaboard. Rock bass have been stocked in states both east and west of their native range.

In the southern half of its range, the rock bass thrives in clear, warmwater streams with rocky bottoms. These streams produce the largest fish.

Fishermen in the North catch most rock bass in relatively clear lakes with moderate vegetation. Fish in weedy lakes seldom reach acceptable size.

Rock bass in northern lakes spawn from late May to late June, usually in water from 65° to 70°F. But in southern streams, they spawn in March and April at substantially lower temperatures, generally 55° to 60°F. They build saucer-shaped nests near rocks, weeds or woody cover. Most nest on sand or gravel bottoms in water only 1 to 4 feet deep. Unlike sunfish, they seldom nest in colonies.

ROCK BASS differ from warmouth and other true sunfish (page 21) in that they have six spines on the anal fin instead of three. Each scale below the lateral line has a dark spot, forming eight to ten rows of horizontal lines.

Primarily bottom feeders, rock bass will take insects on the surface, especially in streams. They usually feed during the day.

Rock bass in both lakes and streams spend most of their time in a relatively small area. In late fall, they become nearly dormant, feeding very little once the water temperature drops below 45°F.

STREAMS. In spring, rock bass may leave their home territory to find a suitable spawning area. Look for spawners in eddies just off the main channel, below rock ledges and undercut banks, and just downstream of dams, rocks and logs.

After spawning, rock bass use the same type of cover but in deeper water. Strong sunlight will force them into deep pools or heavily-shaded areas. But they leave cover in early morning or evening to feed in shallow riffles or in the upper portions of pools where current carries in food. This pattern continues into fall.

Weather has little impact on rock bass in streams. On cloudy days, or when runoff muddies the water, the fish do not hold as tight to cover.

NATURAL LAKES. Rock bass spawn along sand or gravel shorelines, usually near emergent vegetation like bulrushes. Anglers also look for overhanging branches, fallen trees, brush and large boulders where spawning fish can find shade.

In summer, rock bass school on structure in deeper water, usually from 10 to 20 feet. Look for rocky reefs and points, or humps with sand or gravel bottoms. The fish also hold along submerged weedlines, often intermingling with sunfish.

Rock Bass Range

Rock bass edge back into shallow water in fall, but seldom move as shallow as in spring.

COMMON FOODS of rock bass include crayfish and other items too large for most panfish. They also feed on aquatic insects, minnows and other small fish, fish eggs, snails and small crustaceans.

Fishing for Rock Bass

When other fish stop biting, the feisty rock bass often saves the day. One of the most aggressive panfish, it will strike a variety of baits and lures.

As its name implies, the rock bass prefers rocky bottoms. But it also inhabits weedy or brushy areas. In lakes, look for them around submerged rock piles, on rocky points and along weedlines. In streams, they prefer deep eddies with rocks or logs for cover.

The techniques used to catch sunfish in lakes work equally well for rock bass. In fact, many sunfish anglers consider rock bass to be pests, because they often beat sunfish to the bait. Rock bass have larger mouths than sunfish and require bigger hooks.

Stream fishermen usually drift downstream in a small boat or canoe until they spot a deep hole or eddy likely to hold rock bass. Many prefer to fish in waders so they can work a spot thoroughly. Some anglers tie the canoe to their waist and keep it in tow while they wade. Then, they can climb back in quickly and resume floating.

Many stream fishermen use hellgrammites, the larvae of the dobsonfly. One creel census on a midwestern stream found hellgrammites to be the most effective bait for rock bass, outfishing even worms and crayfish.

Popular stream-fishing lures include straight-shaft spinners, spinnerbaits, jigs and small crankbaits. Many anglers tip their lures with small pieces of crayfish tail or worms.

Unlike sunfish, rock bass rarely bite during the winter months. They begin feeding actively in spring, once the water has warmed to 50°F. In lakes, fishing peaks during the spawning period when both males and females strike almost anything tossed near them. The fish bite through summer, but are more difficult to find because they scatter and form loose schools. In streams, rock bass are easiest to find and catch during summer, when they concentrate in deep pools.

Rock bass bite best during the day. But in clearwater lakes, they may continue to feed for several hours after dark.

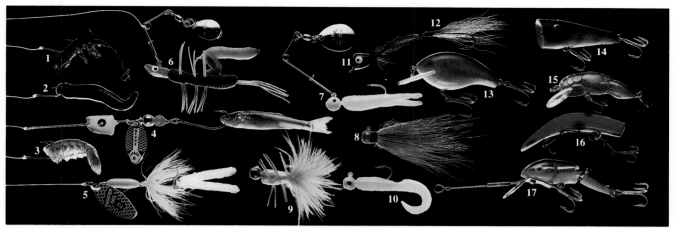

LURES AND BAITS for rock bass include: (1) hell-grammite on #6 hook, (2) leech on #8 hook, (3) crayfish tail on #4 hook, (4) Lusox with minnow, (5) Rooster Tail® with pork rind, (6) Ugly Bug™ with piece of nightcrawler, (7) Beetle Spin™, (8) bucktail jig, (9) Fuzz-E-Grub®, (10) Twister® Teeny, (11) popper, (12) streamer, (13) Teeny-R®, (14) Creek Chub® Plunker, (15) Teeny Wee Crawfish™, (16) Flatfish, (17) Cisco Kid.

How to Use a Spinner-crayfish Combination

PEEL the shell from a crayfish tail, then slice the meat lengthwise to form two strips. If the tail is large, cut the strips in half. Tip a small spinner with pieces of the crayfish meat.

CAST the spinner into the upstream end of a pool or eddy. Reel slowly across current, using a stop-and-go retrieve. Rock bass often follow the lure a long way. An erratic action may cause them to strike.

Other Rigs for Rock Bass

TIP a spinner-jig combination with a small minnow or a 1-inch piece of nightcrawler. A flat-headed jig has a good swimming action in current and its rubber legs give it a lifelike appearance.

PUSH a #4 hook through the middle of a small night-crawler. Add enough split-shot to keep the bait near bottom. Let the worm tumble downstream as if it were being carried by the current.

WHITE PERCH lack stripes. They have the narrowest tail of all the temperate basses. The back may vary from olive to silvery gray to almost black; the sides range from pale olive-green to silvery white. The head and lower jaw of white perch have a bluish lustre during the spring spawning period.

All About White Perch

The name white perch causes confusion among some fishermen, especially those accustomed to calling crappies by that name. To complicate matters, the white perch is not a true perch, but a member of the temperate bass family. Its close relatives include white, yellow and striped bass.

White perch live in fresh, salt and brackish waters. They are mainly found in estuaries along the Atlantic Coast, but also thrive in many inland lakes connected to estuaries. Stocking programs in New York and the New England states have created land-locked populations of white perch in many lakes and reservoirs.

The biggest white perch come from large estuaries and lakes with expanses of warm, shallow water. But many ½- to 1-pound white perch are taken from small lakes and ponds. The world record, 4 pounds, 12 ounces, was caught in Messalonskee Lake, Maine in 1949.

ESTUARIES. In spring, sea-run white perch and fish that live in estuaries swim up coastal rivers to spawn. They scatter their eggs in tributary streams, in feeder creeks and ditches flowing into the tributaries, and in the main stem of the river. Most fish spawn in fresh water, but some in brackish water. Spawning begins when the water temperature reaches about 46°F and peaks at 55°F, slightly before striped bass spawn in the same waters.

After spawning, white perch move back to brackish water in the lower end of the tributary or into the main river channel. Most school around shallow

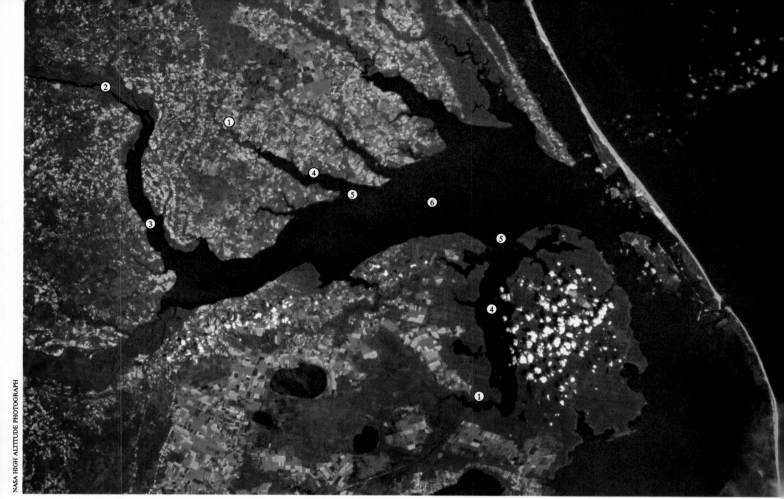

SPAWNING AREAS in estuaries include: (1) upper ends of tributaries and creeks, (2) upper portion of main river. In summer, look for perch in (3) deep areas in the upper river. In fall, many move back into the (4) tributaries. In late fall and winter, they school near the (5) mouths of the tributaries and in (6) the main channel.

shoals, weedlines and brushy shorelines. Some white perch return to the sea.

In fall, many fish migrate back into the streams and shallow ditches. In early winter, they return to the deeper parts of the main channel. However, they will move onto shoals during mild weather.

Throughout the year, white perch in estuaries usually remain close to bottom. The fish cruise along rocks or mud-gravel areas, where they consume large quantities of shrimp and crabs in addition to small fish and insects.

LAKES AND RESERVOIRS. Landlocked populations of white perch spawn in tributaries that feed lakes and reservoirs, generally below the first major dam. If there are no streams, they deposit their eggs in shallow bays. In reservoirs, they sometimes spawn in the upper ends of creek arms. Spawners prefer murky water with a slight current. After spawning, the fish return to the main body of the lake. Look for them near mid-lake shoals in 10 to 20 feet of water or along windswept shorelines. Starting in early summer, packs of white perch herd baitfish to the surface or into small bays or coves. Surface-feeding is most common on cloudy days, usually early or late in the day. The schools tend to work the same areas for several consecutive days, a pattern that continues well into fall. On bright, sunny days, the fish feed in deep water.

In late fall, white perch move to deeper water, often 30 feet or more. Reservoir fish commonly form large schools in the lower part of the lake.

White perch go into a state of semi-hibernation during winter. They remain deep and rarely feed.

In spring, landlocked white perch feed mainly on insect larvae, especially mayfly nymphs. Later, they switch to small fish like smelt, alewives, yellow perch and even their own young. By fall, young baitfish have become too large for the perch, so they eat insects, water fleas and freshwater shrimp.

White Perch Range

127

Fishing for White Perch

Fishermen line the streambanks each spring when white perch swim upstream to spawn. Most anglers prefer live bait, especially worms. They still-fish on bottom, suspend the bait from a float, or cast with a spinner-worm combination. Small white jigs also account for many white perch. Fly-fishing with streamers is another popular and effective technique.

On coastal waters, most fishermen turn their attention to other species once the spawning run is over. Estuary fishing picks up again in fall, when white perch return to the same streams and channels where they spawned. But the fish do not run upstream as far as they did in spring. Fishermen use the same rigs and techniques as they did during the spawning period.

Fishermen on inland lakes and reservoirs catch white perch through summer and well into the fall. In summer, troll with spinners and worms to find the fish. When you locate a school, stop and cast with a spinner or a white jig. White perch spook even more easily than white bass, so cast to the edge of the school rather than to the center. You can stay farther from the school by attaching a clear plastic float ahead of your lure for extra casting distance.

Lights attract white perch on summer nights. Bait a #6 hook with a worm or minnow and let it sink slowly into the lighted area.

In fall, when landlocked white perch move to deeper water, try vertical jigging with a lead-head jig, vibrating blade or jigging spoon. Work the lure near bottom, but occasionally lift it higher to catch suspended fish.

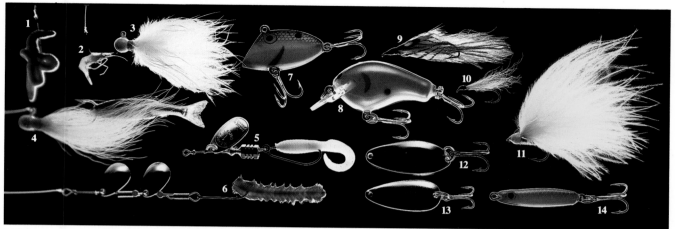

LURES AND BAITS for white perch include: (1) garden worm, (2) grass shrimp, (3) Maribou Jig, (4) bucktail jig with minnow, (5) Comet® Combo, (6) True-Spin with seaworm, (7) Bayou Boogie, (8) Kill'r "B", (9) Gray Ghost, (10) Mickey Finn, (11) marabou streamer, (12) Little Cleo®, (13) Dardevle®, (14) Salty Dog Spoon.

Where to Catch White Perch

SMALL STREAMS, man-made channels and marshy creeks connected to estuaries draw large numbers of white perch in spring. Look for fish in slow-moving stretches.

TAILRACES concentrate white perch swimming upstream to spawn. Fish gather in tight schools in eddies below bridge piers and large boulders.

How to Fly-Fish for White Perch

FLY-CAST for white perch by wading upstream while quartering your casts up-current. Strip in line to avoid slack as the fly drifts downstream. When the fly starts to drag in the current, pick up the line and cast again. Most fly fishermen use 7- to 8-foot rods, No. 5 or No. 6 sinking fly line and small, colorful streamers.

Fliers

Sunfish anglers in the Southeast sometimes catch fliers while fishing sluggish waters clogged with vegetation. But only a few waters contain enough good-sized fliers to provide quality fishing.

A member of the sunfish family, the flier is sometimes called the *round sunfish* because of its plate-like shape. Fliers average only 5 to 6 inches in length, but a few fish reach 8 inches. There is no official world record, but a 1-pound, 4-ounce flier was caught in a South Carolina pond in 1978.

Fliers spawn earlier than most other sunfish, usually when the water temperature reaches 62° to 64°F. They nest in colonies, so spawning time offers the best opportunity to catch numbers of keeper-sized fish.

Flier Range

Young fliers feed heavily on tiny crustaceans; older fish eat mosquito larvae and other insects as well as crustaceans.

Most panfish anglers use baits and lures too big for fliers. The fish will rise to a small dry fly or popper. They will also take a wet fly or a tiny bit of worm.

FLIERS have olive-green sides with horizontal rows of brown spots, giving the fish a speckled appearance. A dusky, wedge-shaped bar extends below the eye of most individuals. The fins are often banded or barred in dark brown. Fliers have a large mouth; the upper jaw extends nearly to the middle of the eye. The anal fin is nearly as long and large as the dorsal fin, so the fish's profile more closely resembles a crappie than a sunfish.

SACRAMENTO PERCH have mottled sides varying in color from brown and white to black and silver. The sides often have several irregular vertical bars. The gill cover has a black spot.

Sacramento Perch

The only sunfish native to the region west of the Rockies, Sacramento perch can survive in waters too alkaline for other gamefish. They seldom thrive in lakes with large numbers of predator fish. Unlike other sunfish, they do not guard their nests, so predators can wipe out the eggs and fry.

Sacramento perch spawn in water about 71°F, often depositing their eggs next to boulders. They bite through the nesting period. In summer, look for them around rocky humps or ledges, or over sand-gravel bottoms. Sacramento perch feed mainly on small fish. They average about 1 pound, but occasionally exceed 3 pounds. The world record, 4 pounds, 9 ounces, was caught in Pyramid Lake, Nevada in 1971.

Sacramento Perch Range

Wet flies and nymphs, like a #6 wooly worm, will catch fish in most waters. Creep the fly slowly along bottom or retrieve it with a slow jigging action. Minnows usually work better than worms.

Rio Grande Perch

Rio Grande perch live only where water temperatures never fall below the low 50s. They thrive in rivers and reservoirs, especially in spring-fed areas with a constant temperature or around heated discharges. They are rarely found in lakes or ponds not connected to flowing water.

In most waters, Rio Grande perch average ½- to ¾-pound, but they sometimes exceed 2 pounds. Favorite foods include insect larvae and small fish. They also eat the eggs of popular gamefish like largemouth bass and bluegills, often destroying the nests.

Spawning occurs at temperatures of about 70°F. Both parents guard the nest and will attack anything that comes near, including the feet of swimmers. Despite their aggressive nature, Rio Grande perch shy away from unusual disturbances. They inspect baits closely and often ignore artificial lures. Small crayfish and worms work best.

Rio Grande Perch Range

RIO GRANDE PERCH have iridescent blue spots on their sides and long, flowing fins. At spawning time, the front of the body becomes a shade of light cream. Adult males have a steeply humped forehead.

Ice Fishing

Equipment for Ice Fishing

To someone who has never tried ice fishing, standing on a frozen, windswept lake may seem cold and forbidding. But ice fishing can be enjoyable if you have the right clothing and equipment.

Veteran fishermen wear layers of clothing rather than a single, heavy layer. They start with insulated underwear, add a wool shirt and pants, and a down coat. Many anglers prefer snowmobile suits. The suits keep out the wind, can be worn over relatively light clothing, and can be easily removed if the weather warms. Keep your extremities warm by wearing a stocking cap, felt-lined boots and *choppers*, leather mittens with removable cloth liners.

Take along a towel for drying your hands. Wet hands chill quickly. Once your fingers begin to numb, fishing becomes nearly impossible. Some anglers carry pocket hand warmers; others use catalytic heaters, lanterns or cans filled with charcoal.

Many ice fishermen use some type of shelter to keep warm. Ice houses, called *shacks* or *shanties*, vary from portable canvas enclosures to carpeted houses as large as a living room. Anglers often equip their shacks with gas, oil or wood-burning stoves.

Some anglers make portable chairs with wooden runners and storage compartments for their fish and gear. Other fishermen simply load their bait, rods and other tackle into a 5-gallon plastic pail which doubles as a seat. Then they put the pail and any other ice-fishing gear on a small, plastic sled that can be easily towed across the ice.

A chisel works well for chopping through a few inches of ice, but when the ice gets thick, you will need some type of drill. A sharp auger can cut through a foot of ice in seconds. If you drill many holes, there is no substitute for a power auger.

Cutting a hole with a dull auger is almost impossible. You can sharpen a cup-style drill with a special hone that clips onto the blade. But sharpening an auger with removable blades is more difficult. Most fishermen replace the blades each season rather than trying to sharpen them. But you can extend the life of your blades with a sharpening steel.

How to Measure Depth Through the Ice

POUR water onto the ice, then place the transducer of a portable flasher in the water. The signal will pass through clear ice, enabling you to read the depth and find fish.

FILL a plastic bag with antifreeze. Use a rubber band to secure the bag around a gun-type depth finder or a transducer. Place the bag on clear ice and read the depth.

ATTACH a clip-on weight to your hook and lower it to bottom. Lift the weight as far off bottom as you want to fish, then attach a bobber to the line at the surface.

Tips for Cutting a Hole

CHISEL a hole with the flat edge of the blade toward the outside. Loop the strap around your wrist to avoid losing the chisel.

DRILL a hole with a (1) power auger, (2) hand auger or (3) Swedish cup-style drill. Some augers have handle extensions for extra thick ice.

SCOOP up ice chips with a plastic or metal skimmer. If you do not have a skimmer, use a kitchen strainer or a plastic minnow scoop.

How to Keep Ice Drills Sharp

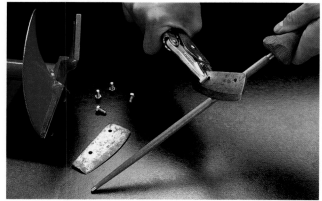

REALIGN the edges of your blades with a sharpening steel. Push the blade down and across the steel, as if cutting a thin slice. Repeat the procedure several times, switching sides of the blade after each stroke.

GREASE your blades to prevent them from rusting. Even a small amount of rust greatly reduces their cutting power. Some fishermen pack a layer of grease into the blade guard for extra protection.

Tackle for Ice Fishing

JIGGLESTICKS include: (1) basic peg model, (2) rod and plastic reel with screw-type drag, (3) rod and built-in reel with line threaded through the rod, (4) rod with large, ice-proof guides and spin-cast reel.

Most panfish anglers use a short, fiberglass rod called a *jigglestick*. About 3 feet in length, jigglesticks usually come equipped with 8- or 10-pound mono wound around pegs on a wood handle. For panfish, most fishermen switch to lighter line.

When using light mono, you risk snapping the line on a good-sized fish. To solve this problem, remove the pegs and add a reel. A reel allows large fish to strip off line and helps you bring your catch up from deep water. Almost any type of reel will work, but a closed-face spinning reel prevents ice and snow from building up on the spool. Use thick, rubberized tape to hold the reel in place and to cover the rod handle. The tape helps to prevent cold fingers.

Many ice fishermen make the mistake of using rods that are too whippy. A flexible rod makes it difficult for a fish to break the line, but also makes it harder to set the hook.

You can make an ice-fishing rod from a broken or discarded tip of a standard fishing rod. Drill a hole in a wooden dowel or a cork rod handle, then glue the rod in place. To prevent ice from building up and restricting line flow, replace the end guide with a larger one.

Water below the ice is generally clear. To avoid spooking panfish, use 4- or 6-pound, low visibility line. Some fishermen prefer line as light as 2-pound test. Detecting a bite is difficult when using twisted or coiled line. Rub the mono across your knee a few times to remove any set.

To detect delicate bites, use a thumbnail-sized float or a *spring-bobber*. A spring-bobber is a sensitive wire attached to the rod tip. The line runs through the eye on the end of the wire. Even the lightest tap causes the wire to twitch.

Most commercial spring-bobbers extend from the rod tip, but experts often attach the wire several inches back from the tip. This way, the wire does not have to bend as much to set the hook.

Floats and Spring-bobbers for Ice Fishing

SMALL FLOATS are usually pegged or clipped to the line. Some can be rigged as slip-bobbers (page 15). For proper balance, attach enough split-shot so the bobber barely stays afloat.

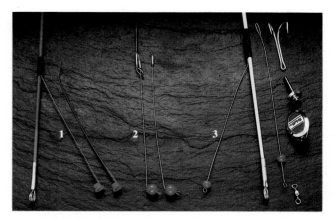

SPRING-BOBBERS include: (1 and 2) commercial types, (3) a homemade model fashioned from the shaft of a strip-on spinner. Some spring-bobbers clip onto the rod tip; others are attached with winding thread or tape.

How to Make a Spring-bobber From a Ball-point Pen

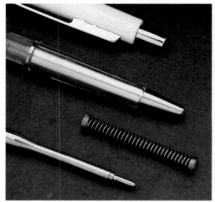

REMOVE the spring from a discarded push-button style, ball-point pen. Or, you can buy a small spring at a hardware store.

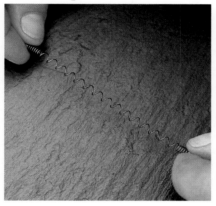

STRETCH the spring to about 5 inches. Bend the end coil so it lies flat and serves as an eye. Straighten the wire on the other end.

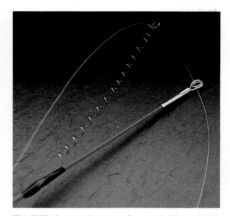

TAPE the spring to the rod. Bend the end guide so it is level with the rod, then thread the line through the eye of the spring-bobber and the guide.

Tips for Bobber Fishing

SQUEEZE a sponge bobber to remove any ice buildup. A coating of ice makes the bobber more buoyant, so it is less sensitive.

PEG a float from the bottom (left). If pegged at the top (right), ice will accumulate faster, eventually tipping the bobber on its side.

GREASE the surface of your float with petroleum jelly to prevent ice from forming. Some fishermen also grease their rod guides.

Ice Fishing Tips

Ice fishermen have devised dozens of clever techniques to make their sport more enjoyable. They use a variety of devices to keep their fishing holes from constantly freezing. They build special chairs that serve as equipment carriers and body warmers. Some anglers equip their shanties with ingenious alarm systems that signal bites.

Safety should always be the foremost concern of ice fishermen. Even the thickest ice can develop cracks or thin spots. If possible, try to follow an old trail rather than blazing a new one.

How to Make a Water Spitter

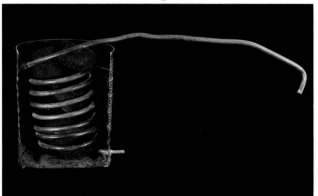

BEND 8 feet of ¼-inch tubing into a 3- to 4-inch wide coil. Place the coil in a 5-inch wide can, drill a hole for the intake, seal the hole with solder and fashion a spout. Add lead to partially sink the can; pile charcoal in the coil.

WATER SPITTERS keep your fishing hole open by squirting an intermittent stream of warm water. When the copper tubing heats up, it draws in cold water from an adjacent hole, warms it and spits it into your fishing hole.

Tips for Keeping the Hole Ice-free

DRILL a hole several inches deep next to your fishing hole. Place a can of charcoal briquets in the shallow hole. Chisel a channel so the warm water can circulate between them.

KEEP out wind-blown snow with a coffee can. Remove the ends, then place the can in the hole. Pile wet snow around the can to hold it several inches above the ice.

CUT a slit in a piece of cardboard, then place the cardboard over the hole. Drop your bait through the slit. This technique also prevents snow from filling the hole.

Tips for Keeping Warm

ICE SHANTIES break the wind and can be warmed easily with a small heater. Be sure to provide enough ventilation to exhaust the fumes.

CARPET REMNANTS help to keep your feet warm. For extra warmth, line the bottoms of your boots with felt inserts.

GAS LANTERNS or catalytic heaters can be placed inside a homemade chair for extra heat. Close the door to prevent heat from escaping.

Safety Tips for Ice Fishing

TEST ice of uncertain thickness by whacking it with a sharp chisel. If the chisel breaks through or the ice cracks, trace your path back to shore.

WEAR ice creepers for better traction. Creepers strap to the bottom of your boots. They have metal teeth that dig into the ice.

AVOID pressure ridges. The pressure of expanding ice causes it to crack and heave, sometimes forming pockets of open water between the chunks.

CARRY spikes as a safety precaution. If you should fall through the ice, jam the spikes in the ice and pull yourself out of the water. Some anglers attach interlocking wood handles.

Ice Thickness Safety Chart

ICE THICKNESS	CARRYING CAPACITY
2 inches	One person walking
4 inches	One person fishing on the ice
5 inches	Snowmobile
8 to 12 inches	Car or light truck

These guidelines from the Minnesota Department of Natural Resources, apply only to clear, blue ice on freshwater lakes. When walking or driving across ice, keep several other factors in mind.

- An ice pack is not uniform in thickness. Inflowing springs bring in warmer water that creates areas of thin ice or pockets of open water. Large schools of fish milling about under the ice also cause thin spots.
- New ice is much stronger than old ice that has been partially thawed and refrozen. Dark, honeycombed ice is the weakest.
- Ice near shore is weaker than mid-lake ice, especially in late winter.
- River ice varies greatly in thickness, depending on the current.

Ice Fishing for Sunfish

Ice fishermen catch more sunfish than any other type of panfish. Anglers have little trouble finding sunfish; the challenge is locating the keepers.

Big sunfish bite best in early winter when the ice is only 2 to 3 inches thick and again just before ice-out.

Sunfish school by size. Large fish generally stay within a foot of bottom, while small sunfish may suspend several feet. If you begin catching small fish, try a different depth or move to another area. Once you find a good spot, look for landmarks to pinpoint the location. Chances are, it will produce fish next season.

Just after freeze-up, look for sunfish in weedy areas less than 8 feet deep. Holes in weedy bays are prime early season locations. Later in the winter, sunfish move to deeper water along drop-offs, but seldom stray far from cover. If the water has enough oxygen, the fish may be as deep as 25 feet. Most species of sunfish require higher oxygen levels than crappies or yellow perch.

Tips for Finding Sunfish

EARLY MORNING and late afternoon offer the best angling, although sunfish bite throughout the day. They seldom bite after dark.

LATE SEASON anglers enjoy fast action. Use a ladder or plank to cross unsafe ice near shore. Check ice thickness before walking to your spot.

LOOK for tips of emergent weeds, such as bulrushes, projecting above the ice. Sunfish often hold near the weedline early and late in the season. They move deeper in mid-winter.

COVER your head with a coat or blanket, then peer down the hole to check for weed growth. Sunfish usually hang in open areas in the weeds. In clear water, you may be able to spot fish.

How to Catch Sunfish

Sunfish generally inspect baits or lures closely, ignoring anything of the wrong size or color. For greatest consistency, use light line, small baits and delicate bobbers. Four-pound monofilament will handle any sunfish. Heavier line usually results in fewer bites.

Most ice fishermen prefer insect larvae for sunfish. Thread them on a #8 or #10 hook, or on a small jig, spoon or teardrop. Favorite lure colors include orange, yellow and chartreuse. When hooking in-

sect larvae, tear the skin slightly so the juices ooze into the water. The scent attracts sunfish.

Spring-bobbers work better than standard floats for signalling sunfish bites, which may be very subtle. A sunfish sometimes grabs the bait without moving the wire. But when you lift the rod, the wire bends from the weight of the fish. Other times, fish will push the bait upward, relieving tension on the wire. Another advantage of a spring-bobber: you can easily change depth without stopping to adjust a float.

How to Customize a Sunfish Rod

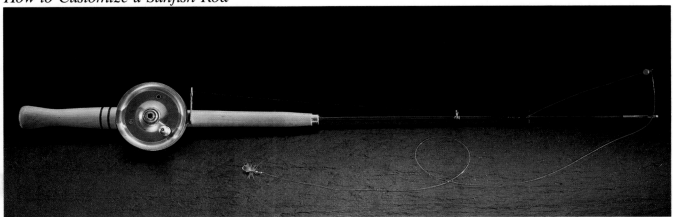

ICE-FISHING RODS for sunfish should be moderately stiff. Bend the end guide so it lies flat. Then, attach a spring-bobber so the eye on the spring lines up with the end guide. Tape on a small metal or plastic reel, or a spin-cast reel to store line and provide a drag. Thread 4-pound mono through the spring-bobber and then through the end guide. Tie on a small lure. Do not add split-shot unless necessary to reach bottom.

How to Detect a Bite With a Spring-bobber

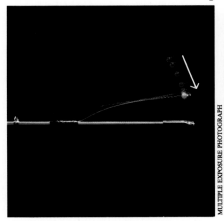

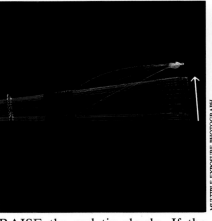

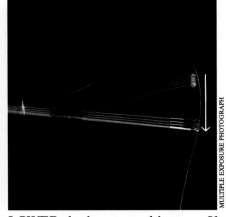

JIGGLE the lure, then stop for a few seconds. Watch the spring-bobber closely. Even a subtle bite will pull the wire downward.

RAISE the rod tip slowly. If the spring-bobber does not move upward at the same rate as the rod tip, a sunfish has taken the lure.

LOWER the lure toward bottom. If the line goes slack when you drop the rod tip, chances are a fish has grabbed the sinking lure.

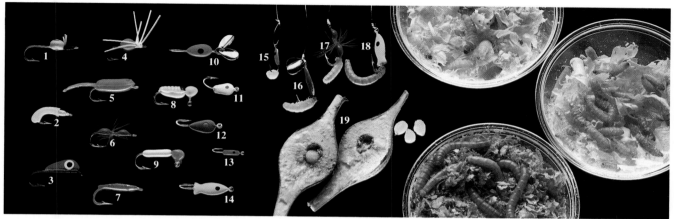

LURES AND BAITS include: (1) Jig-A-Spider, (2) Purist, (3) Chippy, (4) Skin-Yas, (5) Flavored Mouse, (6) Panti® Ant, (7) Moon Glitter, (8) Hott Head, (9) Rat Finky, (10) Fairy, (11) Nubbin, (12) Tear Dot, (13) Speck, (14) Chubby, (15) goldenrod grub, (16) waxworm, (17) silver wiggler, (18) mealworm, (19) goldenrod gall.

Tips for Catching Sunfish

LOOK for patches of snow when the ice is clear. The patches provide shade and reduce spooking. Some anglers spread black plastic on the ice.

ATTACH your lure with a loop knot (page 12). This allows the lure to swing freely, providing extra action when you jiggle the rod.

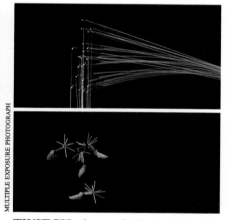

TWITCH the rod tip rapidly for several seconds. The action attracts sunfish. The fish almost always strike when the lure stops moving.

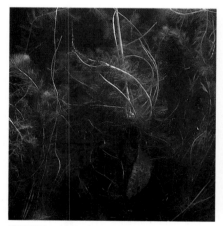

OPEN a hole in weeds by swinging a heavy weight in a circle. Sunfish move in and feed on organisms churned up by the disturbance.

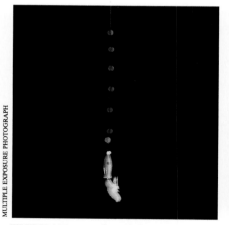

THREAD a colored bead on your line. A sharp twitch moves the bead up the line, then it slides down slowly, attracting sunfish.

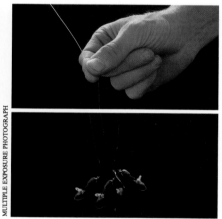

ROLL the line between your fingers to make the lure spin rapidly. When sunfish are fussy, this technique may work better than vertical jigging.

Ice Fishing for Crappies

Crappies inhabit deeper water than most other panfish. In mid-winter, they may be found at depths of 30 feet or more. They usually hang near structure, but may suspend just off structure or in open water. Crappies suspend farther off bottom than other panfish, sometimes rising 15 to 20 feet.

Early and late winter offer the best crappie action. Look for the fish around their usual springtime haunts in water 15 feet or shallower. They prefer a weedy area near the top of a drop-off. Just after freeze-up, fishermen catch crappies in water as shallow as 3 feet.

Crappies are more sensitive to light than other panfish, so cloudy weather usually means better fishing.

They often go on a feeding binge one to two hours before a snowstorm. But the clear, bright skies following a cold front usually slow fishing. Crappies form dense, suspended schools in deeper water and refuse to bite.

Many crappie experts use portable depth finders to locate likely spots. The units save time because you can sound through the ice rather than drill holes to check the depth. You can also spot suspended crappies by sounding through the ice.

If you do not have a depth finder, continually adjust the depth of your bait until you find fish. At times, crappies pack into extremely tight schools. To catch these fish, you must find the exact spot.

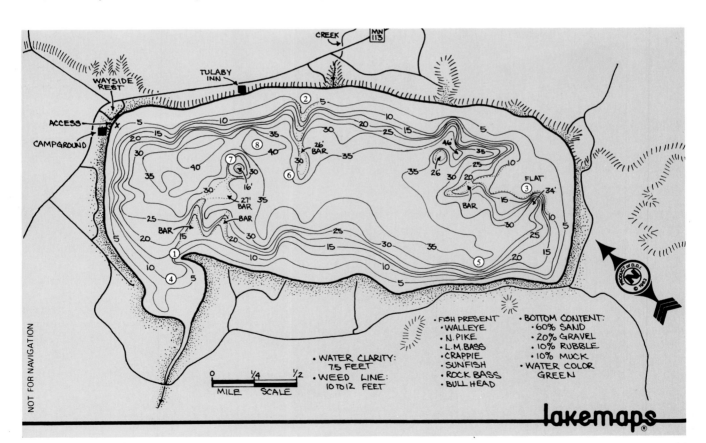

LAKE MAPS help anglers find crappies. Early and late winter spots include: (1) shallow shoreline points, (2) shallow submerged points, (3) edges of flats near deep water, (4) shallow bays. Mid-winter spots include: (5) sharp shoreline breaks, (6) deep extensions of submerged points, (7) mid-lake humps, (8) suspended over deep hole.

NIGHTTIME is often best for crappie fishing, especially in clear lakes. To attract crappies, set a lantern on the ice. The light should not beam down the hole, because it may spook the fish. Crappie fishing usually peaks during the two-hour period after dusk. The fish start to bite again an hour or two before dawn.

How to Catch Crappies

A small minnow dangled below a tiny bobber undoubtedly accounts for more wintertime crappies than any other technique. An active, 1½- to 2-inch minnow usually works best. When fishing is slow, some anglers switch to larval baits like waxworms, goldenrod grubs, maggots and mayfly nymphs, often sold as mayfly *wigglers*.

Most fishermen use larvae to tip small jigs or teardrops. Crappies do not rely on scent as much as sunfish, but the larvae often seem to help. Jigs with soft plastic molded around the hook also work well. Crappies evidently mistake the plastic for real food.

Fishermen sometimes have trouble hooking crappies because the fish mouth the bait before they swallow it. When your bobber goes under, wait a few seconds to set the hook. If you miss the fish, wait longer the next time. If you still cannot hook the fish, switch to a small bait or try a jigging lure.

When fishing is fast, a minnow-like jigging lure or a small spoon may catch several fish in the time it takes to catch one on live bait.

Popular Crappie Rigs

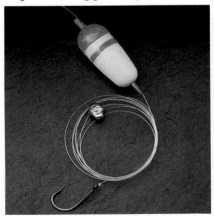

STANDARD RIGS include a peg bobber, enough split-shot for balance and a #4 or #6 short-shank hook. Most anglers use 4- or 6-pound line.

SWIVEL RIGS prevent line twist when jigging. Splice a swivel into the line about 8 inches above the hook; add a small bead and slip-sinker.

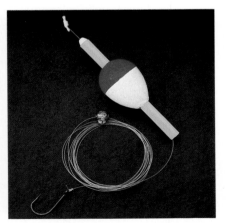

SLIP-BOBBER RIGS work well for deep water, but only when temperatures are above freezing. With ice on the line, the bobber cannot slide.

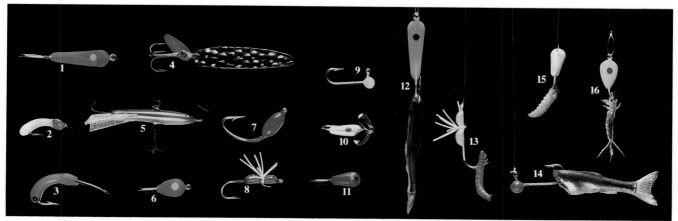

LURES AND BAITS for crappies include: (1) Crappie Rocket, (2) Purist, (3) Rembrant, (4) Swedish Pimple®, (5) Rapala® Jigging Lure, (6) 3-D, (7) Carlson, (8) Ant, (9) Balls-O-Fire, (10) Moxy, (11) Jig-A-Bitzi, (12) minnow, (13) mealworm, (14) rear portion of minnow, (15) waxworm, (16) mayfly nymph.

How to Jig for Crappies

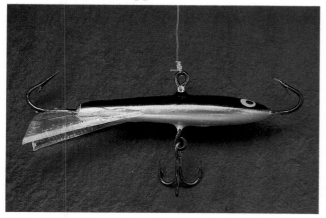

TIE a Jigging Rapala® directly to your line. Most fishermen use 8-pound monofilament. Lighter line may snap when you set the hook. Lower the lure to about 1 foot off the bottom.

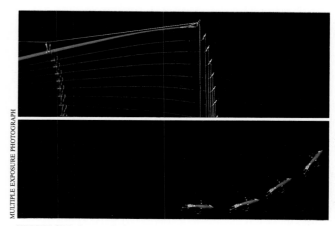

MULTIPLE EXPOSURE PHOTOGRAPH

TWITCH the rod sharply to make the lure dart forward. Wait until the lure settles to rest, pause several seconds, then twitch again. Crappies generally strike during the pause. Set the hook immediately.

Tips for Catching Crappies

STORE leftover minnows in a perforated can. Attach a rope, sink the can and let the rope freeze in. The bait will be fresh when you return.

FIX the depth when you locate fish by placing a tab-type rubber band around the spool. Then you can easily return your bait to the right depth.

WATCH your line when a fish bites. If the line consistently moves off to the same side, it may indicate the whereabouts of the school.

Ice Fishing for Yellow Perch

Ice fishing for yellow perch peaks just before ice-out when they cruise shallow flats and rock piles. In early winter, anglers on natural lakes catch many perch in the back ends of bays or off shoreline points in water only 4 to 8 feet deep. By mid-winter, most perch have moved to deep water, generally from 20 to 40 feet. They gather along breaklines just off sand or mud flats, often near the base of a drop-off.

Mid-morning to mid-afternoon offers the fastest action. Changing weather conditions have little effect on perch fishing.

Most perch fishermen rate minnows as the best bait. Using a #6 hook, pierce the minnow's back just below the dorsal fin. Use a bobber to suspend the baitfish about 6 inches off bottom. Some anglers prefer to drop a dead minnow to bottom. Perch fishermen often tip artificials with larval baits, worms, marshmallows or perch eyes. Favorite lure colors include silver, red, yellow and chartreuse.

Veteran perch anglers use a unique piece of equipment called a *tube rig*. Attach a short leader to a piece of metal tubing, bait with a minnow or perch eye, and drop the rig to bottom in deep water. The heavy tube stirs up the sediment, attracting perch. Let the rig rest on bottom and lift periodically to see if a perch has taken the bait.

SAND-GRAVEL FLATS in water from 10 to 15 feet deep are prime late winter habitat. Yellow perch prefer a clean bottom that is devoid of weeds, brush, trees or other vegetation.

HONEYCOMBED ICE means good perch fishing. But late winter fishing demands extreme caution. Although the ice may still be over 1 foot thick, there may be scattered weak spots.

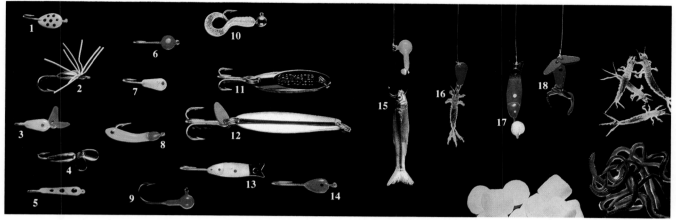

LURES AND BAITS include: (1) Speck'l, (2) Chrome Spider, (3) Jig-A-Flipper, (4) Diamond Back, (5) Slim-Fin, (6) Falcon, (7) Jig-A-Bitzi, (8) Purist, (9) Panfish Assassin, (10) Jiggly, (11) Kastmaster, (12) Swedish Pimple®, (13) Jig-A-Spoon, (14) Darby, (15) minnow, (16) mayfly nymph, (17) piece of marshmallow, (18) red wiggler.

How to Jig With a Swedish Pimple®

RAISE a Swedish Pimple® 2 to 3 feet off bottom, then quickly drop the rod tip. Allow the lure to fall to within 6 inches of bottom. Some anglers tip the lure with a wax-worm or small piece of minnow.

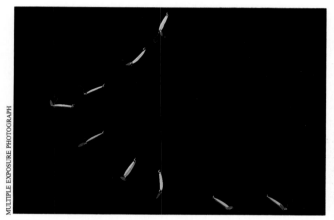

HOLD the rod still as the lure flutters downward. It will flare to one side and then the other before settling to rest. Perch strike after the lure stops moving. Set the hook at the slightest tug.

Tips for Catching Yellow Perch

SCATTER *tip-ups* over a large area to locate perch. When a flag signals a bite, drill a hole nearby and try jigging or bobber-fishing.

LEAVE a hooked perch on the line. The hooked fish may attract other perch and start a feeding frenzy. Fish in a nearby hole.

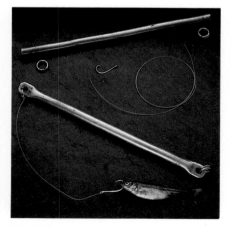

MAKE a tube rig from a 10-inch piece of copper tubing. Drill holes in the flattened ends, then attach split-rings, a leader and a #6 hook.

Ice Fishing for White Bass

White bass can be caught through the ice, but they are difficult to locate in most waters. Begin your search in typical summertime locations, but in slightly deeper water. You may have to explore a large area to find the fish.

Jigging is the most productive white bass technique. A jigging lure will usually catch white bass at two or three times the rate of a plain minnow. Some anglers tip jigging lures with minnows when fishing is slow.

A jigging lure makes it easy to move to a new hole. Simply drop the lure to bottom and begin fishing. If using a minnow, you must stop to reposition the bobber after each move.

White bass continue to feed throughout the year. They may bite at any time of the day. Weather does not seem to affect them as much as it does most other panfish.

Tips for Catching White Bass

LURES include: (1) Rapala® Jigging Lure, (2) Sonar™, (3) Tinsel Tail™, (4) airplane jig, (5) Swedish Pimple®, (6) ice fly, (7) Russian Hook.

LOCATE white bass by drilling a lot of holes. Veteran white bass fishermen use power augers and keep moving until they find the fish.

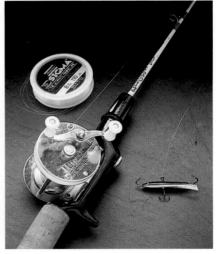

JIG with a short, stiff rod, a bait-casting or spin-cast reel, and 8- or 10-pound line. A reel enables you to bring up fish easily from deep water.

Ice Fishing for Tullibees

Most ice fishermen have never heard of tullibees. But the silvery fish continue to grow in popularity.

Tullibees, or *ciscoes*, live only in deep, cold lakes in the northern states and Canada. In winter, they may be found almost anywhere in a lake. Look for them at depths of 25 to 40 feet in mid-winter. They usually suspend several feet and sometimes as much as 20 feet off bottom. They change depths from day to day, so anglers should experiment. Tullibees move into shallower water just before ice-out, which is the best time to catch them.

Although a tullibee can weigh as much as 5 pounds, it has a tiny mouth. Fishermen use small baits, especially insect larvae. Other popular baits include small minnows and throat latches from fish.

Tullibees bite best during the day. They feed heavily before a storm, but a cold snap drives them into deeper water and slows fishing.

Tips for Catching Tullibees

LURES for tullibees include: (1) Midjet, (2) Tally Jig, (3) Squint (4) Wing Jig, (5) Purist, (6) Hott Head, (7) Rainbow, (8) Tear Dot.

LOCATE tullibees with a depth finder. This flasher shows tullibees suspended from 13 to 15 feet above bottom in 24 feet of water.

MAKE a tullibee rig by first tying on a jigging lure or spoon as an attractor. Add 8 inches of line and a teardrop tipped with a mousie or waxworm.

Ice Fishing for Smelt

In early spring, smelt spawning runs on northern streams draw elbow-to-elbow crowds of dip-net fishermen. Netters fill washtubs with the sleek, silvery fish. Ice fishing for smelt has not gained such widespread popularity, but it is catching on in some regions. In some northern states, the fish have become so popular that ice fishermen hold smelt-fishing derbies.

Primarily saltwater fish, smelt live in estuaries and harbors from Virginia to Labrador. They have been stocked in New England lakes, in Missouri River reservoirs in North Dakota, and in deep, cold lakes scattered throughout the northern states and Canada. In most cases, the fish were stocked to provide food for gamefish. Smelt introduced in a Michigan lake in the early 1900s escaped into Lake Michigan and eventually spread to all of the Great Lakes.

In most waters, smelt average 6 to 8 inches. Anglers refer to a fish larger than 10 inches as a *jack smelt.*

Most of the winter, smelt in deep lakes commonly suspend at depths of 25 to 75 feet. In shallow lakes, look for the fish in the deepest holes. In East Coast estuaries, smelt concentrate in large eddies beneath the ice. The best fishing is during a moving tide. In late winter, smelt often gather near creek mouths prior to their spawning run.

Smelt bite best at night. The most popular baits include tiny minnows and waxworms. In New England waters, many anglers prefer seaworms.

Anglers who work deep water use a specially designed reel with a large spool. Called a *speed reel,* it enables the fisherman to pull in a smelt and return the bait to the depths in seconds. Many anglers prefer multiple hook rigs so they can catch several fish at a time.

The smelt's mouth is lined with hundreds of sharp teeth, making it an efficient predator despite its small size. Natural foods include aquatic worms, larval aquatic insects, and the fry of many types of fish, including lake trout. In some waters, smelt feed heavily on tiny, shrimp-like crustaceans, called *Mysis.*

How to Make and Use a Speed Reel

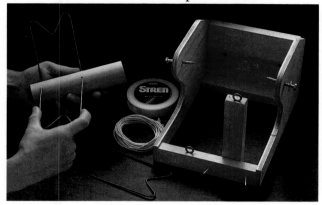

FORCE wire line holders into holes drilled in a 1½-inch wooden dowel. Seat the dowel in the frame so it turns freely. Wind 100 feet of 6-pound mono on the line holders and 25 feet of cord on the dowel. Run the line and cord through small screw eyes.

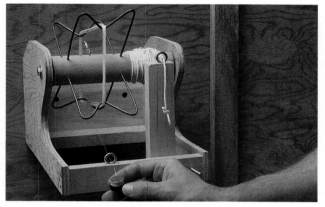

THREAD a small slip-float on the line and add a tandem hook rig with #10 hooks. Do not peg the float to the line or attach a bobber stop. Bait with 1- to 1½-inch shiner minnows hooked through the lips. Lower the rig to the desired depth.

EXPERIMENT with different depths until you find the smelt. Then stretch a rubber band around one of the line holders to fix the depth. This prevents your line from unwinding too far, so you can quickly return your bait to the precise depth after catching a fish.

PULL the cord when you see the float move. You can bring the fish up quickly; a 1-foot pull on the cord will retrieve about 4 feet of line. Grab the smelt to keep it from dropping back into the hole. It may have the bait in its teeth but not be hooked.

Tips for Catching Smelt

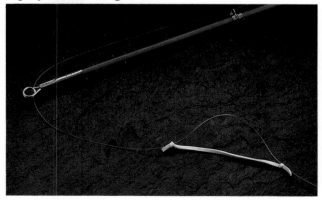

MAKE a bite detector by tying a rubber band to the line in two places, leaving slack line in the middle. When a smelt bites, the rubber stretches.

DIP a ¼-inch piece of seaworm in Mercurochrome™ to give it a dark, reddish color that attracts smelt. Dip the worm again if the color starts to fade.

Panfish Parasites

When panfish anglers clean their fish, they frequently discover parasites. Many fishermen, out of concern for their own health, throw away fish that have black spots on the skin or grubs in the flesh or gills.

Their concern is ill-founded because all parasites of North American fish are harmless to man if the flesh is thoroughly cooked. Very few can be transmitted to humans even when the flesh is eaten raw. Knowledgeable anglers keep fish that have only a small number of parasites, but discard heavily infested fish for esthetic reasons.

Dozens of different parasites infect North American gamefish. Panfish that live near weeds often become infested, because weed-dwelling snails are a link in the life cycle of many parasites. Panfish caught in deep water have fewer parasites, because the fish seldom venture into water inhabited by snails.

The life cycle of the black grub is similar to that of many other parasites. The kingfisher, a fish-eating bird, hosts an intestinal worm whose eggs fall into the water with the bird's droppings. After the eggs hatch, the immature larvae find their way into the intestinal tract of a snail. Several weeks later, the larvae mature into a more advanced form and leave the snail. They attach themselves beneath the scales of a fish, resulting in the commonly seen black spots. The life cycle is completed when a kingfisher eats an infested fish. Other fish-eating birds like herons, gulls and cormorants host other kinds of parasites.

Many anglers believe that fish get parasites only during the hottest part of summer. But fish can carry parasites at any time of the year, even during winter. Ice fishermen often catch yellow perch and sunfish laced with yellow or black grubs.

Game and fish agencies have reduced parasite problems by treating water with chemicals that kill snails. When this link in the life cycle is broken, parasites cannot reproduce. But this temporary solution is very expensive and impractical in large lakes.

BLACK GRUB, the most common parasite of panfish, appears as black spots on the skin. In some cases, the

SKINNING often removes black grubs. But if the fish is heavily infested, some of the parasites may have burrowed into the flesh.

grub may penetrate the flesh, peppering the meat with black specks. The grub itself is white. The black spot is a protective case formed by the fish's body. It is not harmful to humans if eaten.

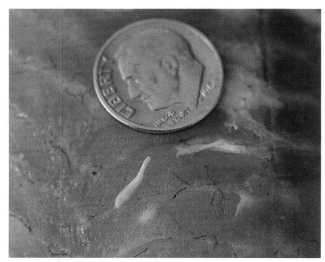

YELLOW GRUB, a common, worm-like parasite, burrows into the muscle and is seldom visible on the body surface. Anglers discover the grub when cleaning their fish.

TAPEWORMS live in the body cavity and internal organs. They do not penetrate the muscle. These flat, whitish worms may grow to a length of 2 to 3 inches.

Index